Science
Inspirations

Dave Rear

S SEIBIDO

photographs by

iStockphoto

Shutterstock

Science Inspirations

To Teachers and Students

Science has the remarkable ability to ignite our curiosity and kindle the flames of inspiration. It unveils the hidden wonders of the natural world, unravels the mysteries of the universe, and shines light on life itself. Science encourages us to question, explore, and innovate. It allows us to dream of new possibilities, whether this is imagining sustainable futures, treating diseases, or venturing into the depths of space. In this book, we look at twenty issues in science and technology that are inspiring people around the world today.

The book is divided into five sections, each covering a different field of scientific exploration. In Section I, we look at Nature and the Environment, answering questions such as whether we should bring back extinct animals and how we can protect our cities from climate change. Section II delves into the world of Humans and Society. We move from the innovative work of a teenage scientist translating sign language to the seemingly mundane – but just as important – issue of how to raise a cat. Section III takes us to Space and Exploration. Are UFOs real? What life-changing discovery did Hayabusa make on Ryugu? Can we grow plants on the Moon? In Section IV, we switch our attention to Health and Medicine. We find out why mosquitoes bite some people more than others and look to the future with microscopic robots that can swim through the bloodstream. In the last section of the book, our focus is on how science is bringing us The Future Now. We hear about Japanese scientists creating robots with living skin and aeronautical companies aiming to produce planes that can fly us to the other side of the world in under an hour.

Each unit has a variety of activities to promote understanding of the topics and development of language skills. Two vocabulary sections introduce and practice key words from the text, extending students' knowledge of scientific terms. The reading passage has two sets of questions, one to assess comprehension of the major themes and the other to encourage a more detailed understanding. There is a writing section that presents important grammatical structures and a listening dictation that encourages students to catch useful expressions and phrases. Finally, students are given the opportunity to discuss their opinions about the topic, the activity scaffolded by a brainstorming exercise to help them generate ideas and vocabulary. Whatever your interest in science, we hope you can find something in this book to inspire you in your own future work. Good luck!

Dave Rear

Table of Contents

Section III: *Space and Exploration*

Section IV: *Health and Medicine*

Section V: *The Future Now*

Extinct No More

Can We Bring Back Mammoths?

もし，あなたが氷河期にタイムスリップできたら，氷に覆われた地球を歩き回るマンモスの群れ
を目にするでしょう。狩猟と温暖な気候のために 1 万年前に絶滅したこの壮大な生き物を，もし
生き返らせることができるとしたらどうでしょう。それは，あり得ない話ではありません。

Key Vocabulary

次の単語について，その定義を結びつけましょう。

1. extinction   **(a)** the smallest living part of an animal or plant

2. primitive   **(b)** a small section of DNA

3. gene   **(c)** the natural environment for an animal or plant

4. preserve   **(d)** a type of animal in danger of dying out

5. cell   **(e)** related to early humans

6. endangered species   **(f)** when an animal no longer exists on Earth

7. habitat   **(g)** to prevent something being damaged

7

When the movie *Jurassic Park* came out in 1993, audiences were excited by the sight of ferocious dinosaurs coming to life on the big screen. The film used computer-generated imagery (CGI) to recreate these giants of the Earth's past, but it also inspired a new question for the human race: Could we bring back dinosaurs for real?

5　To bring a species back from extinction requires two things: a sample of its DNA and a close relative still living today. Unfortunately, scientists have not discovered any DNA from dinosaurs, which died out too long ago for their genes to have survived. They have, however, collected DNA from another great creature that once roamed the Earth: the wooly mammoth. Wooly mammoths existed during the last Ice Age, protected from the
10　cold weather by the thick coat of hair that covered their bodies. Most of them died out 10,000 years ago through a combination of rising temperatures and hunting by primitive humans, though a small population survived until 2000 BC on an island near Siberia.

It is in Siberia that mammoth DNA has been discovered, the freezing temperatures preserving enough of their bodies in ice. Although the cells in these bodies are dead,
15　scientists have been able to read the DNA inside them, making the idea of cloning them a real possibility. The next step to doing so involves combining the mammoth genes with those of their nearest living relative, the Asian elephant, in order to create an embryo.

Ideally, that embryo would be carried in the womb of an elephant, which would give birth in the usual way. The problem is that Asian elephants are endangered, making
20　researchers unwilling to experiment with them. Instead, the aim is to create an artificial womb that would do no harm to a living creature. So far, researchers have only done experiments with mice. Creating a womb large enough to nurture a mammoth is expected to take at least another decade.

🎵 1-07

If they do manage to develop the technology to clone a mammoth, the next question is:

25 Should they? There is still a habitat cold enough for mammoths to live comfortably – Siberia where their DNA was discovered – but there are clearly risks involved with bringing back an animal that has been extinct for so long. What will the effect be on the ecosystem? How will they raise the first generation of mammoths who will not have mothers to teach them the skills of life? And with so many current species threatened

30 with extinction, should we not focus on protecting them rather than bringing back old ones?

🎵 1-08

These are not easy questions to answer. But the idea of mammoths roaming the Earth once more is an exciting one. And, unlike *Jurassic Park*, let's hope this story has a happy ending.

Notes **ferocious** 猛烈な **roam** 歩き回る **embryo** 胚 **womb** 子宮 **nurture** 育てる
ecosystem 生態系

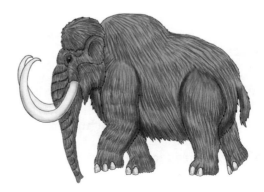

True / False

次の文が本文の内容と一致する場合は T，一致しない場合は F を記入しましょう。

1. (   ) It is currently possible to bring dinosaurs back from extinction.

2. (   ) Some mammoths survived until about 4,000 years ago.

3. (   ) Scientists have collected mammoth DNA but they do not have a living relative.

4. (   ) It is problematic to use living Asian elephants to nurture a mammoth embryo.

5. (   ) There is no place on Earth where mammoths could live comfortably today.

次の質問に英語で答えましょう。

1. What are the two things needed to bring a species back from extinction?

   _____

   _____

2. How long is it expected to be before an artificial womb for mammoths can be created?

   _____

   _____

3. Why would the first generation of mammoths have a particular problem?

   _____

   _____

Vocabulary in Context

次の英文の空所に入れるのに正しい語句を下から選びましょう。

1. Every (　　　　　) in the human body carries DNA.

2. Many species face (　　　　　) due to climate change.

3. Can we find a suitable (　　　　　) for wooly mammoths?

4. Stone Age humans had very (　　　　　) tools.

5. We have to (　　　　　) the rainforest for future generations.

| extinction | primitive | cell | habitat | preserve |

Writing Sentences—Making a Contrast 1

対比を表す表現を学びます。次の英文の (　　) 内の単語を並べ替えて，意味の通る文にしましょう。大文字の語も小文字で記されています。

1. 細胞は死んでいたが，科学者たちは DNA を読み取ることができた。

(the / were / although / dead / cells), scientists could still read their DNA.

(　　　　　　　　　　　　　　　　　　　　　　　　　　　　　　　　)

2. マンモスのクローンを作ることは可能かもしれないが，それをやってみるべきか？

Cloning a mammoth might be possible, (should / try / to / but / do / we) it?

(　　　　　　　　　　　　　　　　　　　　　　　　　　　　　　　　)

3. マンモスを復活させるのは，リスクがあるとしてもワクワクする。

It would be exciting to bring back mammoths, (doing / the / of / risks / despite) so.

(　　　　　　　　　　　　　　　　　　　　　　　　　　　　　　　　)

Listening Summary

 1-09

音声を聞いて，次の英文の空所を埋めましょう。

Bringing back animals from extinction ¹⁾_____ the movie
Jurassic Park. But what if we could do it for real? Surprisingly, it is not an impossible
dream. To recreate ²⁾_____, you need a sample of its DNA
and a close living relative. Unfortunately, no DNA has ³⁾_____
for the dinosaurs of *Jurassic Park*; however, we do have DNA from another great
animal of the past: the wooly mammoth. We also have ⁴⁾_____,
the Asian elephant. So, can and should we bring mammoths back? There are two
problems. One is that scientists ⁵⁾_____ experiment with
Asian elephants, which are an endangered species, so they have to create an artificial
womb for the mammoth embryo. ⁶⁾_____ that we can't
predict the consequences of returning an extinct animal to a modern ecosystem. The
technology for doing so, however, could be ready soon.

Express your Ideas

A. クラスメートと話し合って，円の中にあるテーマに関係している単語をリストアップしてみましょう。

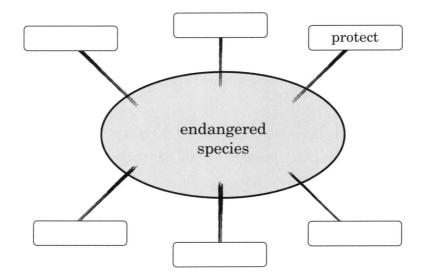

B. 次の英文を読んで，自分の考えを書きましょう。

1. Why are some species on Earth in danger of becoming extinct?

   _____

   _____

   _____

2. How can we protect endangered species?

   _____

   _____

   _____

That Sinking Feeling

UNIT 2

Cities Returning to the Sea

地球温暖化による海面上昇が，沿岸部に住む人々に脅威を与えていることはよく知られています。しかし，海岸沿いの都市は別の問題にも直面しています。それは地盤沈下です。地盤沈下の原因と解決策を探ります。

Key Vocabulary

次の単語について，その定義を結びつけましょう。

1. threaten   **(a)** to sink or go lower

2. survival   **(b)** to take something out

3. satellite   **(c)** continuing to live after a dangerous situation

4. subside   **(d)** an object in space used to receive and send signals

5. regulation   **(e)** to influence, have an effect on

6. extract   **(f)** to be likely to cause harm or damage

7. affect   **(g)** a rule or law

1-11

One of the most well-known effects of global warming is rising sea levels, which threaten the survival of small island nations like Kiribati, Tuvalu, and the Marshall Islands. But Pacific islands are not the only places facing the threat of environmental change. New data has revealed that a shocking number of large coastal cities are sinking into the
5 ground up to several centimeters each year.

1-12

The data has come from a large-scale study of coastal cities spread across six continents. The research team from the University of Rhode Island in the U.S. used satellites to map the height of the ground in each city from 2015 to 2020 by sending microwaves toward the Earth and measuring the timing and intensity of the waves as they bounced back to
10 space. Accurate up to one millimeter, the method allowed the researchers to examine how the ground changed during those five years.

1-13

The results showed that some cities, like Tianjin in China, Karachi in Pakistan, and Manila in the Philippines, are sinking up to five centimeters per year, while many more are dropping by more than a centimeter. Rising sea levels are one cause of the problem,
15 while another is that the land itself is sinking. "Understanding that second part of the problem is a big deal," the lead researcher commented. The team believes the sinking is due to people pumping groundwater out for drinking and other uses, which causes the soil beneath to subside.

1-14

The combination of rising sea levels and sinking land has serious consequences for
20 people living in coastal areas. In the short term, they face higher risks of floods from both rivers and seas, and in the long term they may have to leave their homes completely if the land starts to disappear beneath the water. The problem is especially serious in southeast Asia, where over 185 million people live in coastal floodplains, around 75 percent of the global total.

CD 1-15

25 The good news is that the groundwater issue is a problem that can be fixed if cities are willing to change their behavior. The Indonesian capital of Jakarta, for instance, was sinking by nearly 30 centimeters a year until new government regulations limited how much groundwater could be extracted. The same is true of Tokyo, parts of which subsided almost four meters during the 20th century before strict new rules were introduced.
30 Today, the sinking has been almost completely prevented.

CD 1-16

The researchers from the University of Rhode Island hope their study will raise awareness of this serious global problem. Regions affected by sinking can share their local solutions with other cities and bring about positive change. While global warming is not an issue that will disappear any time soon, coastal sinking might be one thing we have the power
35 to fix.

Notes **coastal city** 沿岸都市　**microwaves** マイクロ波　**intensity** 激しさ，強度　**groundwater** 地下水　**floodplain** 氾濫原

True / False

次の文が本文の内容と一致する場合は T，一致しない場合は F を記入しましょう。

1. (　　) Along with small island nations, large cities are also affected by environmental change.

2. (　　) The University of Rhode Island study measured microwaves going from and back to satellites.

3. (　　) Land sinking in cities is not caused by human activity.

4. (　　) There are both short-term and long-term consequences to the land sinking problem.

5. (　　) Tokyo is still sinking seriously each year.

Understanding Details

次の質問に英語で答えましょう。

1. Exactly how accurate was the method used by the University of Rhode Island study?

_____

_____

2. Which part of the world is most seriously affected by land sinking?

_____

_____

3. How quickly was Jakarta sinking before it created new regulations?

_____

_____

Vocabulary in Context

次の英文の空所に入れるのに正しい語句を下から選びましょう。

1. Global warming will (　　　　　) the Earth in many ways.

2. That moving object in the night sky is a (　　　　　).

3. The (　　　　　) of the human race may depend on the actions we take.

4. The government introduced a new (　　　　　) to clean the water supply.

5. We cannot (　　　　　) any more minerals from this area.

survival	satellite	regulation	extract	affect

Writing Sentences — Making a Contrast 2

対比を表す表現を学びます。次の英文の (　　) 内の単語を並べ替えて，意味の通る文にしましょう。大文字の語も小文字で記されています。

1. マニラの地下は今も沈下しているが，東京は何とか問題を解決している。

The land under Manila is still sinking, (to / has / managed / whereas / Tokyo / solve)
the problem.

(　　　　　　　　　　　　　　　　　　　　　　　　　　　　　　　　　　　　　　)

2. この問題については，私たちの努力にもかかわらず進展がない。

(all / efforts / of / our / spite / in), we have not made progress on this issue.

(　　　　　　　　　　　　　　　　　　　　　　　　　　　　　　　　　　　　　　)

3. 地球温暖化の解決は難しいだろう。しかし，あきらめてはいけない。

It will be difficult to solve global warming. (up / must / we / give / however / not).

(　　　　　　　　　　　　　　　　　　　　　　　　　　　　　　　　　　　　　　)

Listening Summary 1-17

音声を聞いて，次の英文の空所を埋めましょう。

We are used to hearing about the problem of [1]_____
caused by global warming, but a recent study of coastal cities on six continents
revealed another worrying trend. Many cities [2]_____
into the ground by as much as five centimeters a year. The study was carried out
[3]_____ that bounced microwaves down to the Earth and
measured their timing and intensity when they came back. The research team
believes the sinking is due to people taking groundwater out for drinking and other
uses, which causes the [4]_____. If not stopped, it could
[5]_____ and even force people to leave their homes. The
good news is that it [6]_____ if cities change their behavior.
Jakarta and Tokyo are good examples of what can be achieved.

A. クラスメートと話し合って，円の中にあるテーマに関係している単語をリストアップしてみましょう。

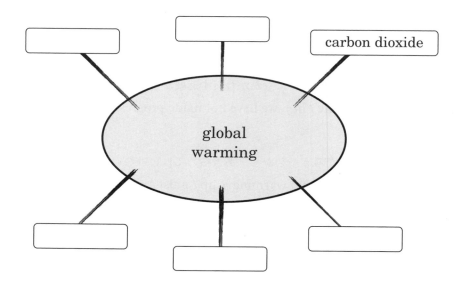

B. 次の英文を読んで，自分の考えを書きましょう。

1. What other effects on Earth does global warming cause?

_____

_____

_____

2. How should we try to solve the problem of global warming?

_____

_____

_____

The Meat Problem

Solutions from the Lab

食用の動物を供給する食肉産業は，森林破壊や地球温暖化など，多くの環境問題を引き起こしています。そのような中，近年，バイオテクノロジー企業が，家畜を殺す必要がない肉の生産を始めました。培養肉と呼ばれるこの肉によって，多くの環境問題が解決されるかもしれません。

Key Vocabulary

次の単語について，その定義を結びつけましょう。

1. livestock
2. consumption
3. deforestation
4. emissions
5. sterile
6. bacteria
7. accelerate

(a) sending out gas or heat into the air

(b) very small living things that sometimes cause disease

(c) the using or eating of something

(d) to make something happen faster

(e) the cutting of trees in a forest

(f) completely clean without any bacteria

(g) animals kept on a farm like cows or pigs

1-19

Human beings eat an incredible amount of meat. Currently, almost 130 million chickens, 4 million pigs, and 1 million cows are killed every day for food. By weight, 60 percent of the mammals on Earth are livestock, 36 percent are humans, and only 4 percent are wild. The problems caused by meat consumption are well-known: deforestation to clear
5 space for pasture; methane emissions from livestock that contribute to global warming; and health issues resulting from over-eating. More and more people are turning to vegetarianism or veganism as an answer, but for those unwilling to quit their meat habit, another solution may be on its way: "cultured" meat grown in a laboratory.

1-20

Cultured meat is different from plant-based meat made from products like soy, peas,
10 beans, and mushrooms. It is based on cells taken from a living animal which are placed in a warm tank containing nutrients like salt, proteins, and carbohydrates. Known as a bioreactor, the tank enables the cells to grow into meat. Unlike plant-based meat, which, although delicious, tends to have a different texture and flavor to animal meat, cultured meat should taste and feel as though you are eating the real thing. Furthermore, since it
15 is grown in a sterile environment, there is less chance of bacteria entering the product, a problem with normal meat from livestock.

1-21

Scientists believe that if enough cultured meat can be grown, it could provide a solution to the environmental problems caused by the meat industry. A recent study by the Potsdam Institute for Climate Impact Research (PIK), for example, found that if we
20 changed 20 percent of our meat to cultured meat by 2050, deforestation would be halved. Methane emissions would also be cut significantly. The ideal situation, of course, would be an even higher percentage than that.

1-22

In 2020, Singapore became the first country to allow cultured meat to go on sale. The "chicken bites," produced by a U.S. company called Eat Just cleared all the country's
25 food safety regulations, allowing it to be sold in restaurants and shops. Currently, Eat Just's products are more expensive than normal meat since production is still on a small

scale; but once they are able to increase the size and number of their bioreactors, the company says that eventually they should become cheaper. Moreover, with more and more companies joining the cultured meat industry, it is likely that more efficient

30 methods for growing lab-based meat will be found, accelerating its progress toward becoming a practical alternative to the traditional meat industry.

1-23

Biotech methods for food production require electricity to power the process, so reducing the CO_2 impact of electricity generation is also important. But if we can continue to innovate, one day we may reach a time where the killing of animals for food becomes a

35 thing of the past.

Notes

mammal 哺乳類, 哺乳動物   **pasture** 牧草地   **methane** メタン
cultured meat 培養肉   **nutrient** 栄養素   **protein** タンパク質
carbohydrates 炭水化物

True / False

次の文が本文の内容と一致する場合は T，一致しない場合は F を記入しましょう。

1. (   ) Cultured meat could be a good solution for people who don't want to give up eating meat.

2. (   ) Cultured meat should taste different from existing plant-based meat.

3. (   ) Current livestock meat is produced in an environment without bacteria.

4. (   ) In the future, cultured meat should become less expensive than now.

5. (   ) More companies are becoming involved in the cultured meat industry.

Understanding Details

次の質問に英語で答えましょう。

1. What is the tank called in which cultured meat is grown?

   _____

   _____

2. What kind of regulations have to be cleared in order to sell cultured meat in shops and restaurants?

   _____

   _____

3. Why is it important for the cultured meat industry to reduce CO_2 emissions of power generation?

   _____

   _____

Vocabulary in Context

次の英文の空所に入れるのに正しい語句を下から選びましょう。

1. This is a (   ) environment so everybody must wear gloves and masks.

2. The global (   ) of meat is rising year after year.

3. The meat industry is responsible for the (   ) of the Amazon.

4. Wash your hands regularly to prevent the spread of (   ).

5. It is not only carbon dioxide (   ) that cause global warming but also methane.

consumption	deforestation	emissions	sterile	bacteria

Writing Sentences — Expressing Causes and Reasons

原因や理由を表す表現を学びます。次の英文の（　　）内の単語を並べ替えて，意味の通る文にしましょう。大文字の語も小文字で記されています。

1. 食肉の消費によって引き起こされる環境問題を無視することはできない。

We cannot ignore the environmental problems (from / consumption / our / which / result) of meat.

(　　　　　　　　　　　　　　　　　　　　　　　　　　　　　　　　　　　　　)

2. 技術の進歩により，培養肉が現実のものとなってきた。

(advances / to / technology / in / due), cultured meat has become a reality.

(　　　　　　　　　　　　　　　　　　　　　　　　　　　　　　　　　　　　　)

3. 森林破壊が急速に進んでいるので，早急に解決策を見出さなければならない。

We must find a solution soon, (proceeding / so / deforestation / since / is) rapidly.

(　　　　　　　　　　　　　　　　　　　　　　　　　　　　　　　　　　　　　)

Listening Summary

🎧 1-24

音声を聞いて，次の英文の空所を埋めましょう。

Human beings appear to be addicted to meat. More than 130 million chickens, pigs, and cows are killed every day for food. Our [1)]_____ causes serious problems, including deforestation, global warming, and health issues. Some people turn to vegetarianism or veganism, but are there [2)]_____? The answer might involve technology as companies are developing a way of producing meat without [3)]_____. So-called "cultured meat" is grown in a laboratory from [4)]_____ from living animals, which are mixed with proteins and other nutrients. Unlike plant-based meat, cultured meat has the same [5)]_____ as real meat. Although it is expensive at the moment, if production can be scaled up, eventually it should [6)]_____ than normal meat from livestock. A solution to our meat addiction could be on the way.

Express your Ideas

A. クラスメートと話し合って，円の中にあるテーマに関係している単語をリストアップしてみましょう。

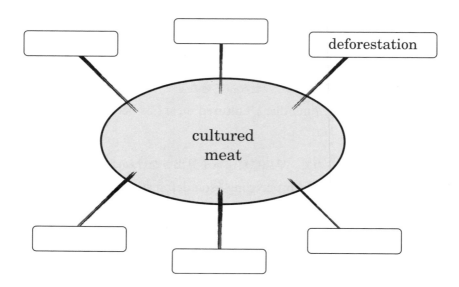

B. 次の英文を読んで，自分の考えを書きましょう。

1. Why do people decide to become vegetarians or vegans?

_____

_____

_____

2. Would you like to try cultured meat?

_____

_____

_____

UNIT 4

The Science of Size

Why Aren't Land Mammals Bigger?

アフリカゾウは大きな動物ですが，過去の巨大恐竜と比べると比較的小さな動物といえます。なぜゾウより大きな陸生哺乳動物はいないのでしょうか。その答えは，哺乳動物の体の機能に関係しています。

Key Vocabulary

次の単語について，その定義を結びつけましょう。

1. constant   **(a)** an animal that eats only plants

2. reptile   **(b)** deadly, causing death

3. ecosystem   **(c)** staying at the same level

4. herbivore   **(d)** to develop gradually over a long time

5. digestion   **(e)** all living things within an environment

6. fatal   **(f)** the process of breaking down food in the stomach

7. evolve   **(g)** an animal such as a crocodile or snake

1-26

What is the largest land mammal alive today? The answer, of course, is the African elephant. An average male elephant is 3.3 meters in height and weighs six tons, an impressive size especially if you are fortunate enough to stand close to one. But by the standards of other creatures on Earth, an elephant isn't all that special. The largest
5 dinosaur that ever lived is thought to have been 26 meters in length with a weight of almost 60 tons, while a blue whale, also a mammal but one which lives in the sea, can weigh up to 150 tons. By the standards of these two giants, the African elephant is just a baby.

1-27

So, why aren't there any land mammals larger than an elephant? Why can't they reach
10 the size of the great dinosaurs that roamed the Earth millions of years in the past? The answer is fairly simple: heat. Mammals are *endotherms*, which means they have to keep their bodies at a constant warm temperature. Reptiles, in contrast, are *ectotherms*: their body temperature varies with the environment. Ectotherms are not able to be active in the cold like mammals, but they also save a lot of energy by not generating their own
15 heat. As Felisa Smith, a researcher of ancient ecosystems, says, "If you take a reptile and mammal of the same size, the mammal needs 10 times more energy than the reptile does."

1-28

This energy comes from food, and it is no coincidence that the largest mammals are all herbivores, making use of plants for their body fuel. Large herbivores have to eat more or
20 less constantly to get the energy they need, but the process of digestion, carried out by bacteria in the stomach, also produces heat. While some heat is necessary for survival, too much can be fatal. For a large endotherm, Smith says, "it's kind of a disaster."

1-29

Mammals have evolved methods to get rid of some of the heat that builds up. Elephants, for example, have huge ears with blood vessels that help to release heat into the air. They
25 can also wave their ears backwards and forwards to act as a cooling fan. But once a mammal reaches a certain size, requiring it to digest a truly enormous amount of food, it would be impossible to keep itself cool.

1-30

Heat limits small mammals too. The smallest mammal living today is the bumblebee bat, which, at less than two grams, is about the size of the bee after which it is named.
30 Scientists believe it would be impossible for a mammal smaller than that to survive since it would lose too much heat to the air. From two grams to six tons is an impressive range of size for the most successful type of animal in the world today, but unfortunately it can't get any larger than this.

Notes **endotherm** 内温動物　**ectotherm** 外温動物　**blood vessel** 血管
bumblebee bat キティブタバナコウモリ

True / False

次の文が本文の内容と一致する場合は T，一致しない場合は F を記入しましょう。

1. (　　　) The elephant is the largest mammal in the world.

2. (　　　) A mammal requires more energy than a reptile.

3. (　　　) Harmful bacteria mean that mammals often have problems with their stomachs.

4. (　　　) If a mammal was too large, it would have to consume too much food to be able to stay cool.

5. (　　　) The heat issue limits how small mammals can be as well as how large.

次の質問に英語で答えましょう。

1. What advantage do endotherms have compared to ectotherms?

   _____

   _____

2. What do elephants have in order to keep themselves cool?

   _____

   _____

3. Why might a blue whale be able to grow so large even though it is a mammal? (Use your judgment. This answer is not directly in the article.)

   _____

   _____

Vocabulary in Context

次の英文の空所に入れるのに正しい語句を下から選びましょう。

1. The fragile (   ) of the rainforest must be protected.

2. Although it is hard to notice, animals on Earth continue to (   ).

3. Some animals eat stones to help with (   ).

4. The largest (   ) in the world today is the saltwater crocodile.

5. Body heat is essential to a mammal's survival, but too much can be (   ).

reptile	ecosystem	digestion	fatal	evolve

Writing Sentences — Expressing Effects and Results

効果や結果を表す表現を学びます。次の英文の (　　) 内の単語を並べ替えて，意味の通る文にしましょう。大文字の語も小文字で記されています。

1. 哺乳類は内温動物なので，天候に左右されずに活動することができる。

   Mammals are endotherms, (be / they / so / active / regardless / can) of the weather.

   (　　　　　　　　　　　　　　　　　　　　　　　　　　　　　　　)

2. 大型の哺乳類は，ほぼ絶え間なく食べ続けなければならないので，消化による熱が発生する。

   Large mammals have to eat almost constantly, (the / to / leading / of / generation) heat from digestion.

   (　　　　　　　　　　　　　　　　　　　　　　　　　　　　　　　)

3. 熱を持ちすぎると命にかかわるので，哺乳類はあまり大きくなれない。

   Too much heat is dangerous with the (grow / mammals / that / result / cannot) too large.

   (　　　　　　　　　　　　　　　　　　　　　　　　　　　　　　　)

Listening Summary

🔊 1-31

音声を聞いて，次の英文の空所を埋めましょう。

The largest land mammal in the world is the elephant, but 1)_____ sea mammals like the blue whale or reptiles like dinosaurs, they are relatively small. Why are there no land mammals larger than an elephant? The answer has to do with heat. Mammals are warm-blooded animals, which means they 2)_____ a lot of food to keep their energy levels high enough. But the 3)_____ food creates heat. Heat is necessary for survival, but too much is fatal. Large mammals 4)_____ ways to release some of this heat, such as the huge ears of an African elephant, but if they grew too large, they would have to consume so much food that it would be impossible to stop their 5)_____ from rising too high. Heat is also the reason why mammals do not 6)_____ the tiny bumblebee bat.

Express your Ideas

A. クラスメートと話し合って，円の中にあるテーマに関係している単語をリストアップしてみましょう。

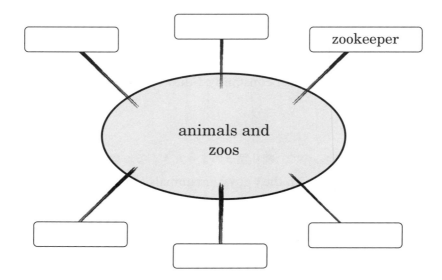

animals and zoos

zookeeper

B. 次の英文を読んで，自分の考えを書きましょう。

1. Do you have a favorite wild animal or animals? Why do you like them?

_____

_____

_____

2. Do you think we should keep wild animals in zoos?

_____

_____

_____

UNIT 5

Helping the Deaf

The Teen Who Translates Sign Language

インドのある10代の若者が，手話を理解できない聴覚障害をもつ人々のコミュニケーションを支援する発明を思いつきました。彼のアプリはスマートフォンにダウンロードすることができ，手話をスクリーン上でテキストに翻訳することができます。どのような仕組みになっているのでしょう。

Key Vocabulary

次の単語について，その定義を結びつけましょう。

1. compete   **(a)** to think of a new idea

2. come up with   **(b)** the purpose of an object or device

3. inequality   **(c)** to find a particular thing or person in a group

4. identify   **(d)** a period when you are made to wait

5. enable   **(e)** to allow, make possible

6. delay   **(f)** to take part in a race or competition

7. function   **(g)** when things are not fair for everyone

🎧 1-33

Every year, teens from around the world compete for a prize at the largest high school research competition, the Regeneron International Science and Engineering Fair held in the United States. In 2022, a 17-year-old inventor from Bangalore, India, unveiled a product that impressed the judges with both its practicality and its awareness of an issue
5 that few people ever consider. Nand Vinchhi was brainstorming with his friends when he came up with an idea for translating sign language into written text to allow deaf people to communicate more easily with those of normal hearing ability.

🎧 1-34

"I've always been super interested in a better education system for everyone, especially in my country where there's a lot of inequality," the teen says. "I wanted to do something
10 through technology that would help."

🎧 1-35

As a coder rather than an engineer, Nand wanted to create something that didn't require a new device, which could be expensive to buy and unlikely to spread widely enough to be useful. So he developed an app that could be downloaded onto an ordinary smartphone. The app reads the hand movements made by a person using American Sign
15 Language (ASL) and translates them into text on the screen in real-time.

🎧 1-36

It took Nand just a few months to make his first version of the app. It wasn't all plain sailing, but whenever he hit a problem he couldn't solve, the teen would go to bed, often finding that when he woke up the next morning, the solution had come to him. The hardest part, he says, was finding what approach to take. He decided to begin by
20 considering what parts of the body are important in signing, such as a person's fingers, hands, and arms. Then, using a machine learning program, he taught a computer to identify those key parts in videos, creating a data set of different movements and positions. An algorithm he then developed enabled the program to analyze the differences between them and build up a vocabulary of ASL signs.

1-37

25 The app can now translate with up to 90 percent accuracy, the time from signing to translation taking about three-tenths of a second. This is only a tenth of a second longer than the typical speech delay in video calls, and Nand believes that in the future the app could be built into video conference systems like Zoom. He also aims to add more sign languages, such as British and Chinese, to improve the app's range and function.

 1-38

30 As well as helping deaf people to communicate, Nand hopes that his invention will also be useful to people trying to learn sign language, since it gives them an effective way to practice the vocabulary they learn. The Indian teen is determined to reduce inequality in the world one sign at a time.

Notes

unveil 発表する，初公開する　**practicality** 実用性
coder プログラマー（コードを書く人）
plain sailing 順調な（進行），容易なこと　**algorithm** アルゴリズム

True / False

次の文が本文の内容と一致する場合は T，一致しない場合は F を記入しましょう。

1. (　　) Not many people had thought about the problem that Nand decided to solve.

2. (　　) One advantage of Nand's invention is that many people already own the device it uses.

3. (　　) The first step Nand took was developing an algorithm to analyze differences between ASL signs.

4. (　　) At the moment, the time from signing to translation with Nand's app is too long.

5. (　　) There is more than one type of sign language in the world.

次の質問に英語で答えましょう。

1. What social problem in India does Nand mention?

   _____

   _____

2. What did Nand often do when he had trouble with his invention?

   _____

   _____

3. How else might the app be useful in addition to helping deaf people to communicate?

   _____

   _____

Vocabulary in Context

次の英文の空所に入れるのに正しい語句を下から選びましょう。

1. The new robot should (   ) us to increase the speed of our production.

2. We must (   ) some new ideas to expand our business.

3. We have added an extra (   ) to our app.

4. To solve the problem, we must first (   ) what caused it.

5. There is too much (   ) in our society.

| come up with | inequality | identify | enable | function |

34

Writing Sentences — Expressing Conditionals

仮定法を表す表現を学びます。次の英文の（　　）内の単語を並べ替えて，意味の通る文にしましょう。大文字の語も小文字で記されています。

1. このアプリがうまく機能すれば，聴覚障害をもつ人々の生活向上に貢献できるかもしれない。

(functions / the / if / well / app), it could help to improve the lives of deaf people.

(　　　　　　　　　　　　　　　　　　　　　　　　　　　　　　　　　　　　)

2. この発明は，人々が簡単に買えるほど安くなければ，役に立たない。

The invention won't be useful (is / enough / unless / for / it / cheap) people to buy it easily.

(　　　　　　　　　　　　　　　　　　　　　　　　　　　　　　　　　　　　)

3. 新たな問題にぶつからない限り，来年には製品を発売できるはずだ。

(don't / hit / as / long / we / as) any new problems, we should be able to release the product next year.

(　　　　　　　　　　　　　　　　　　　　　　　　　　　　　　　　　　　　)

Listening Summary

 1-39

音声を聞いて，次の英文の空所を埋めましょう。

Indian teenager Nand Vinchhi was ¹⁾_____ friends when he came up with an idea for helping people with hearing difficulties. The idea was to ²⁾_____ to translate sign language into written text to make it easier for deaf people to communicate. As a programmer, Nand didn't want his invention ³⁾_____ an expensive new device that people would have to buy; instead, he created an app that could be downloaded onto an ordinary smartphone. Using ⁴⁾_____, he trained a computer to recognize the key body parts used in sign language and ⁵⁾_____ to build up a vocabulary of signs. His invention impressed the judges at the world's largest high school ⁶⁾_____, the Regeneron International Science and Engineering Fair held in the United States.

Express your Ideas

A. クラスメートと話し合って，円の中にあるテーマに関係している単語をリストアップしてみましょう。

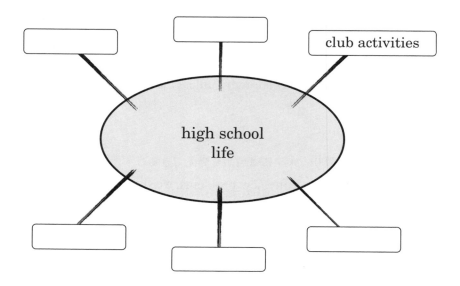

B. 次の英文を読んで，自分の考えを書きましょう。

1. Did you enjoy your high school life? What were the good and bad points?

_____

_____

_____

2. Why did you become interested in science and technology as a teenager?

_____

_____

_____

Feline Truths

How to Make Your Cat Love You

世界で最も人気のあるペットは猫と犬ですが，その行動様式は全く異なります。犬は常に飼い主を愛しているように振る舞い，一方の猫は喜ばせるのが難しい生き物です。では，猫の世話をする秘訣は何でしょうか。この質問に対する答えは，私たちの期待と反するものかもしれません。

Key Vocabulary

次の単語について，その定義を結びつけましょう。

1. loyal
2. hostile
3. feline
4. stroke
5. evaluate
6. initiate
7. interaction

(a) to start or begin
(b) always supporting
(c) to consider how good something is
(d) connected with cats
(e) talking or acting with someone
(f) to gently move your hand over a surface
(g) aggressive or unfriendly

1-41

Are you a cat person or a dog person? The world's two most popular pets are very different in their personalities and behavior. While dogs tend to be warm, friendly, and loyal, bounding to the door to welcome their owners home as soon as they hear the click of a key in the lock, cats are more likely to be cool, calm, and independent. They usually
5   only come running when they want to be fed. With a dog, owners don't have to work too hard to be loved. Man's best friend loves anyone who loves them back. Cats, however, are more difficult to please. They can be loving and affectionate to some and cold and hostile to others.

1-42

A question many cat owners have, therefore, is: What is the best way to make your cat
10   love you? Other than feeding and caring for them, is there anything humans can do to improve their relations with their feline companions? The answer, according to a recent study, is surprising and perhaps a little disappointing. Generally speaking, cats prefer people who don't like cats.

1-43

The reason is that cats are very sensitive about where people stroke them. There are "red
15   areas" where they hate to be touched, including the stomach and the base of the tail, "yellow areas," like their legs and back, that they will tolerate but not enjoy, and "green areas," such as under their chin or behind their ears, where touching is welcomed.

1-44

In the study, which was published in the journal *Scientific Reports*, 120 people with varying degrees of experience with cats were given the opportunity to spend five minutes
20   in a room with three cats. Researchers recorded and evaluated how the person behaved and how the cats reacted. What they found was that the cats responded best to people who waited for the animals to come of their own accord and touched them only to a minimum degree. Naturally, these tended to be the people with little experience with cats and little interest in playing with them. Cat owners and cat lovers, on the other
25   hand, were more likely to initiate contact themselves and to stroke the cats in the red or yellow areas they did not like. They also had a tendency to pick up or hold the animals,

something cats do not enjoy since they prefer to be in control of when and how interaction occurs.

🎵CD 1-45

30 For cat owners, the study offers some valuable lessons, even if they are ones they might not want to hear. But what should you do if you're the kind of person who likes to pay your pet a lot of attention? There might be a solution that is simple enough to try. You could think about getting a dog.

> **Notes**
>
> **bound to** 〜に駆け寄る
> **man's best friend** 人間の最良の友 [欧米では愛犬の意味として使われるフレーズ]
> **affectionate** 愛情の深い，優しい **tolerate** 許容する，我慢する
> **of their own accord** 自発的に，自分の意志で

True / False

次の文が本文の内容と一致する場合は T，一致しない場合は F を記入しましょう。

1. (   ) It is easier to make a dog love you than a cat.

2. (   ) Cats don't really like to be stroked on their backs.

3. (   ) Cats react best when you pay them lots of attention.

4. (   ) People who have lots of experience with cats are more likely to know how to please them.

5. (   ) The results of the study should be popular with cat owners.

Understanding Details

次の質問に英語で答えましょう。

1. For what reason do cats usually come running to their owners, according to the article?

   _____

   _____

2. Where are the "green areas" for a cat?

   _____

   _____

3. How long did each participant in the study spend with the three cats?

   _____

   _____

Vocabulary in Context

次の英文の空所に入れるのに正しい語句を下から選びましょう。

1. We need to (   ) our performance so far.

2. He has been a (   ) customer of ours for many years.

3. It will be interesting to observe the (   ) between the two animals.

4. The hairs standing up on the animal's back signaled its (   ) attitude.

5. This material feels so smooth when you (   ) it.

| loyal | hostile | stroke | evaluate | interaction |

Writing Sentences — Comparative Adjectives

比較級の形容詞を学びます。次の英文の（　）内の単語を並べ替えて，意味の通る文にしましょう。
大文字の語も小文字で記されています。

1. 猫は犬よりずっと自立している。

Cats (more / than / are / independent / much) dogs.

(　　　　　　　　　　　　　　　　　　　　　　　　　　　　　　　　　)

2. 猫は犬ほど注目を浴びたいわけではない。

Cats are not (in / attention / interested / as / getting) as dogs.

(　　　　　　　　　　　　　　　　　　　　　　　　　　　　　　　　　)

3. 自立心が強いので，犬よりも猫の方が世話がしやすい。

Because they are more independent, it is (than / to / after / easier / a / look / cat) a dog.

(　　　　　　　　　　　　　　　　　　　　　　　　　　　　　　　　　)

Listening Summary 1-46

音声を聞いて，次の英文の空所を埋めましょう。

Cats and dogs are the most popular pets in the world, but they have very 1)_____. Dogs tend to have a natural love for their owners while cats can be more picky about who they give their affection to. A recent research study set out to discover what 2)_____ from people was most likely to bring 3)_____ from our feline friends. In the study, human participants spent five minutes in a room with three cats, interacting with them as they wanted. The researchers found that people with experience with cats were 4)_____ stroke the animals in so-called "red areas" or "yellow areas," where cats do not like 5)_____. Those with less interest in cats, on the other hand, touched them in "green areas" or not at all. This is the behavior the cats responded to 6)_____. So, what is the secret to making cats love you? Perhaps it is not to love them too much!

Express your Ideas

A. クラスメートと話し合って，円の中にあるテーマに関係している単語をリストアップしてみましょう。

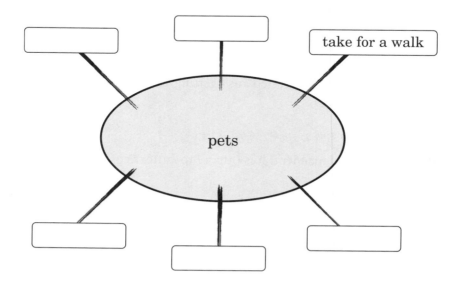

take for a walk

pets

B. 次の英文を読んで，自分の考えを書きましょう。

1. Do you have a pet? If so, what kind of pet? If not, what kind of pet would you like?

_____

_____

_____

2. Do you think children should have a pet as they grow up? What can a pet teach children?

_____

_____

_____

Mind Control

Does Hypnosis Really Work?

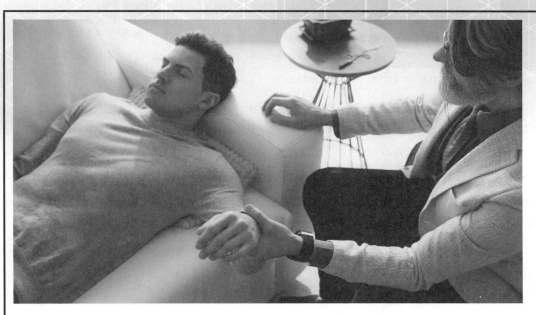

催眠術とは本当に実在するものなのでしょうか。もしそうなら，私たちが催眠術にかかるとき，脳では何が起こっているのでしょう。私たちは催眠術師が望むことを拒むことはできないのでしょうか。催眠術という不思議な科学について，たくさんの疑問があります。その疑問の答えを見つけてみましょう。

Key Vocabulary

次の単語について，その定義を結びつけましょう。

1. phenomenon   **(a)** relating to beliefs about right and wrong

2. conscious   **(b)** an event in nature or society

3. anxiety   **(c)** medical treatment that involves cutting into the body

4. surgery   **(d)** worry or fear

5. anesthesia   **(e)** a negative or bad result

6. morally   **(f)** using a drug so the patient feels no pain

7. ill-effect   **(g)** awake and able to notice things

1-48

Have you ever seen a show in which a magician hypnotizes a member of the audience and has them perform embarrassing acts on stage such as barking like a dog or kissing a total stranger? Have you ever wondered if such shows are real or if they're faked? Let's examine the science of hypnosis to find out.

1-49

5　Hypnosis is not a modern phenomenon. It has been practiced in various forms for centuries, though it wasn't until 1843 that a Scottish doctor named Dr. James Braid popularized the term itself. He was referring to a state of concentrated relaxation in which a person can be guided into doing or saying things their conscious mind would not normally allow. Away from stage shows, it is a valuable technique used by trained
10　healthcare professionals to treat conditions including anxiety, phobias, pain, depression, and stress.

1-50

To treat a patient, a professional will first conduct a questionnaire to see how susceptible they are to hypnosis, as this varies from person to person. Studies show that only about two-thirds of adults can be hypnotized successfully. After that, the hypnotist will ask the
15　patient to imagine a place that makes them feel safe and relaxed before focusing on a particular detail, such as the sound of the waves in the sea or the feel of the sun on their skin. If done right, the patient's physical surroundings will melt away and they will feel themselves transported into the place their minds have conjured. They are now open to the suggestions the hypnotist gives them.

1-51

20　What precisely happens to the brain during this "hypnotic state" is still unknown. Imaging studies have shown that the brain region which helps people switch between tasks quiets down and that it becomes disconnected from another area responsible for self-reflection. It is believed that this is what allows people to lose their usual inhibitions. Researchers have also found that hypnosis can calm brain regions controlling heart rate, blood flow,
25　and breathing, leading to the patient's state of complete physical relaxation. So powerful is this that it has even been used for patients undergoing surgery in place of general

anesthesia. Combining hypnosis with local anesthesia has been shown to produce quicker recovery times, as general anesthesia can bring a stress reaction from the body even though the patient is unconscious.

 1-52

30 So, are hypnosis shows real or faked? Performers claim they are real, the techniques being the same as those used in professional settings. Contrary to what Hollywood may tell us, people cannot be made to do things they are morally opposed to, like violence or murder. Audience members who have experienced hypnosis describe a kind of "out of body" feeling in which they see themselves acting strangely but can't bring themselves to

35 stop. Luckily, there are no lasting ill-effects, except, perhaps, a sense of embarrassment when they watch the recording later.

Notes

popularize 世に広める，流行させる　**phobia** 恐怖症
susceptible 影響を受けやすい（例: susceptible to hypnosis 催眠術にかかりやすい）
conjure 思い描く，思い浮かべる　**self-reflection** 自己反省　**inhibition** 抑制
general anesthesia 全身麻酔　**local anesthesia** 局所麻酔

True / False

次の文が本文の内容と一致する場合は T，一致しない場合は F を記入しましょう。

1. (　　　) The practice of hypnosis was invented in 1843 by Dr. James Braid.

2. (　　　) The majority of adults can be hypnotized.

3. (　　　) Hypnosis does not seem to have any effects on the brain.

4. (　　　) If you are hypnotized, you do not feel any pain.

5. (　　　) Hypnotists cannot make people do things they have a moral reason not to do.

次の質問に英語で答えましょう。

1. Why do hypnotists ask patients to fill out a questionnaire before beginning treatment?

   _____

   _____

2. What physical processes in the body can be changed by hypnosis?

   _____

   _____

3. Why might people recover quicker if they don't receive general anesthesia during surgery?

   _____

   _____

Vocabulary in Context

次の英文の空所に入れるのに正しい語句を下から選びましょう。

1. The patient decided to try hypnosis to treat her (   ).

2. We do not fully understand this (   ) yet.

3. You shouldn't suffer any (   ) after the treatment.

4. He was (   ) of what was happening but didn't feel any pain.

5. The doctor explained to the patient what would happen during the (   ).

phenomenon	conscious	anxiety	surgery	ill-effects

Writing Sentences—Superlative Adjectives

最上級の形容詞を学びます。次の英文の（　）内の単語を並べ替えて，意味の通る文にしましょう。大文字の語も小文字で記されています。

1. このケースは，医師がこれまで見た中で最も難しいものの一つであった。

This case (of / hardest / the / was / one) the doctor had ever seen.

(　　　　　　　　　　　　　　　　　　　　　　　　　　　　　　　　　　　)

2. この新しい治療法は，私が今まで受けた中で最も成功した。

This new treatment was (received / ever / successful / I've / most / the).

(　　　　　　　　　　　　　　　　　　　　　　　　　　　　　　　　　　　)

3. 彼は最も有名な催眠術師である。

He is the (hypnotist / all / famous / of / most).

(　　　　　　　　　　　　　　　　　　　　　　　　　　　　　　　　　　　)

Listening Summary   1-53

音声を聞いて，次の英文の空所を埋めましょう。

When we think of hypnosis, we might imagine a stage performance in which members of the audience are made to carry out embarrassing, if harmless, 1)_____. In fact, however, it is a serious health practice used for the treatment of conditions 2)_____, stress, and phobias. When a person is hypnotized, they enter a state of total relaxation, which 3)_____ to influence them in ways that would be impossible if they were 4)_____. Brain studies show that hypnosis quiets down regions of the brain responsible for multi-tasking and self-reflection; it can also change 5)_____ like heart rate and blood flow. So powerful can its effects be that doctors have even begun to use it as an alternative to general anesthesia. While not everyone can be hypnotized, there is little doubt that it is a 6)_____.

Express your Ideas

A. クラスメートと話し合って，円の中にあるテーマに関係している単語をリストアップしてみ
ましょう。

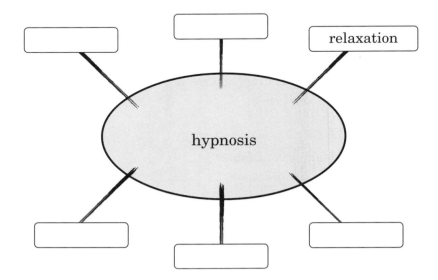

B. 次の英文を読んで，自分の考えを書きましょう。

1. Have you ever seen a hypnotism show on television? What happened in it?

_____

_____

_____

2. Would you be willing to be hypnotized? Why / why not?

_____

_____

_____

UNIT 8

Science for All

The Rise of Citizen Scientists

科学研究は，知識やノウハウを持ったプロの科学者にしかできないと思っていませんか。しかし実際には，一般の人々の協力を必要とするプロジェクトも増えているのです。では，彼ら市民科学者たちはどのように貢献できるのでしょうか。

Key Vocabulary

次の単語について，その定義を結びつけましょう。

1. civilization
2. collaboration
3. contribute
4. astronomy
5. pollution
6. diversity
7. conservation

(a) to provide help with something
(b) many kinds of different people or things
(c) the study of space and stars
(d) the protection of wildlife and nature
(e) working together
(f) damage caused to water, air etc. by harmful substances
(g) an advanced society

1-55

Have you ever thought how amazing it would be to receive contact from an alien civilization? In 2012, the organization responsible for finding intelligent life in space – the Search for Extraterrestrial Intelligence (SETI) – gave people the chance to do just that. After a TED talk calling for collaboration between professional and amateur scientists,
5 members of the public were invited to join SETI in analyzing radio signals from space that were picked up by the organization's radio telescopes. The aim of the project was to find patterns within the signals that might indicate they originated from an alien civilization. While SETI's own computers had algorithms to analyze the signals, some parts of the data were so crowded that it required humans to sort through them. Over
10 74,000 people volunteered to join the project, and, though it did not, unfortunately, find any evidence of extraterrestrial life, it was an excellent example of how ordinary people can contribute to the work of professional scientists.

1-56

While astronomy is perhaps the most exciting area of so-called "citizen science," it is far from being the only one. The *Globe at Night* project, for instance, calls for volunteers to
15 collect data on light pollution using only their smartphone. Participants take pictures of the night sky while recording their observations of how bright or dark their surroundings are. By identifying the star constellations they are photographing, they can compare how the sky looks to how it would look if there was no light pollution. The *Globe at Night* project aims to both collect data and raise awareness of the problem, and it also has a
20 sister project known as *NoiseTube* that does the same for noise pollution.

1-57

Other areas where citizen scientists can contribute are nature and health research. On the *Instant Wild* website, volunteers tag animals in photos taken in the wild, while on the *iNaturalist* site, they can upload their own photos of wildlife and birds. Both of these projects aim to track the diversity of the Earth's ecosystems and contribute to conservation
25 efforts. Gamers, meanwhile, can assist with health research through online games like Foldit and Neureka. In the former, they fold and design proteins for use in drug treatments

and in the latter, they answer questions to help with research into mental health and dementia.

 1-58

You might imagine that, however interesting these projects are, they do not lead to real
30 scientific progress. In fact, however, citizen scientists have made significant discoveries. For example, they were the first to identify a strange purple air glow called STEVE, which is similar to the Northern Lights. They were also the first to find "yellowballs" in telescope images, mysterious space objects that appear when stars are just beginning to form. Considering all the challenges faced by the Earth today, the idea of amateur and
35 professional scientists working together to solve the world's problems is certainly an exciting one.

Notes

extraterrestrial 地球外生物　**radio signal** 電波信号
originate from ～から来る，～に由来する　**constellation** 星座
protein タンパク質　**dementia** 認知症　**Northern Lights** オーロラ

True / False

次の文が本文の内容と一致する場合は T，一致しない場合は F を記入しましょう。

1. (　　　) SETI used both computers and humans to analyze radio signals from space.

2. (　　　) Unfortunately, most of the SETI volunteers were not smart enough to collaborate with the scientists.

3. (　　　) *Globe at Night* and *NoiseTube* both aim to investigate types of pollution.

4. (　　　) Online gamers can contribute to research in both physical and mental health.

5. (　　　) It is unrealistic to expect citizen scientists to make real scientific discoveries.

次の質問に英語で答えましょう。

1. Which organization is responsible for discovering signs of intelligent life in space?

_____

_____

2. On what website do volunteers place pictures they have taken?

_____

_____

3. What is STEVE?

_____

_____

Vocabulary in Context

次の英文の空所に入れるのに正しい語句を下から選びましょう。

1. I hope to (　　　　　) to this new research project.

2. The (　　　　　) of people in our organization helps to generate new ideas.

3. Researchers were delighted to find evidence of an ancient (　　　　　).

4. We must work hard to reduce the problem of (　　　　　) in our cities.

5. Ever since she was a child, she was interested in (　　　　　).

| civilization | contribute | astronomy | pollution | diversity |

Writing Sentences—Using the Passive

受動態を使った表現を学びます。次の英文の（　　）内の単語を並べ替えて，意味の通る文にしましょう。大文字の語も小文字で記されています。

1. この星は，アマチュア天文家のグループによって発見された。

The (group / discovered / by / was / a / star) of amateur astronomers.

(　　　　　　　　　　　　　　　　　　　　　　　　　　　　　　　　　　　　　　　)

2. どこから電波信号が来ているかは知られていない。

It (known / where / is / the / not) radio signals are coming from.

(　　　　　　　　　　　　　　　　　　　　　　　　　　　　　　　　　　　　　　　)

3. 騒音公害の問題は，私たちの努力にもかかわらず，解決されていない。

The problem of noise (not / has / solved / pollution / despite / been) all of our efforts.

(　　　　　　　　　　　　　　　　　　　　　　　　　　　　　　　　　　　　　　　)

Listening Summary

 1-59

音声を聞いて，次の英文の空所を埋めましょう。

Scientific research is not just for professionals. There are a growing number of projects which ¹⁾_____ of ordinary members of the public. One of the most famous was created by SETI in 2012, the aim being to assist the organization ²⁾_____ radio signals from space in the hope of finding one that originated from an ³⁾_____. No alien signals were found, but people ⁴⁾_____ to scientific projects in astronomy, health, and the environment. They can tag or upload ⁵⁾_____ and play online games that add to our knowledge of proteins and mental health. Some citizen scientists have even managed to make ⁶⁾_____. These include the phenomena of "yellowballs" made by distant stars and a strange purple air glow known as "STEVE."

Express your Ideas

A. クラスメートと話し合って，円の中にあるテーマに関係している単語をリストアップしてみましょう。

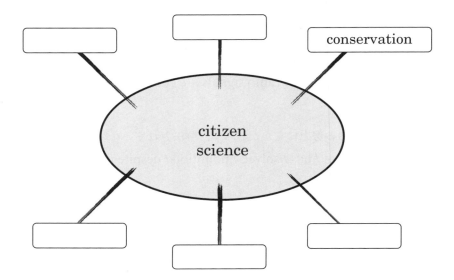

B. 次の英文を読んで，自分の考えを書きましょう。

1. Which of the "citizen science" projects mentioned in the article interests you the most? Why?

   _____

   _____

   _____

2. Do you think games are a good way for people to get new skills or knowledge?

   _____

   _____

   _____

UNIT 9

Real After All

NASA's Growing Interest in UFOs

UFOの目撃者と聞くと，想像力が過剰で信頼性の低い人を連想しがちですが，実際には沢山の UFOが厳粛な軍のパイロットによって目撃され録画されています。これらの飛行物体は何なのか，そしてどこからやって来るのか。アメリカ政府はまさに今，その答えを突き止めようとしています。

Key Vocabulary

次の単語について，その定義を結びつけましょう。

1. fleet   **(a)** the ability to move quickly

2. exclamation   **(b)** to see or notice something

3. agility   **(c)** to decide something is not possible

4. observe   **(d)** words spoken suddenly to express an emotion

5. capable of   **(e)** the meaning of a word in a dictionary

6. rule out   **(f)** having the skill to do something

7. definition   **(g)** a group (of ships)

🎧 **CD** 1-61

Mysterious flashing lights at night. Saucer-shaped ships that hover over the land without sound. Objects that shoot across the sky, diving and changing direction at incredible speeds. Unidentified flying objects, or UFOs, have fascinated human beings for decades, but there is much we don't understand about them. What are they? Where do they come

5 from? What do they want? There is, however, one thing we absolutely do know. UFOs exist. They are real.

🎧 **CD** 1-62

"Look at that thing, dude! Oh my gosh. There's a whole fleet of them."

"Wow, what is that, man? Look at it fly!"

These exclamations came from recordings made by U.S. air force pilots in 2015 when

10 they spotted saucer-shaped objects flying across the ocean, twisting and diving with a speed and agility that no known human technology could manage. The g-forces produced should have torn the aircraft apart and killed whoever was piloting them, and yet these objects were in the sky all day for 12 hours or more. Some even dived into the water and out again.

🎧 **CD** 1-63

15 The UFOs observed in 2015 were by no means unique. In the last 20 years, military pilots have seen – and sometimes recorded – over 400 unidentified objects in the sky. Their reports have been taken seriously enough to inspire investigations at the highest levels of the U.S. government, including the Department of Defense, Congress, and NASA. What these organizations want to find out is not whether the UFOs are real or not

20 – nobody believes the pilots are lying – but what they are. There are three possible explanations. One is that they are new weapons being tested by foreign powers like Russia or China, both of which are known to be working on hypersonic systems capable of flying at over five times the speed of sound. Another is that they belong to the U.S. military itself from secret programs the pilots are not aware of. And the third explanation,

25 of course, is that they are alien ships originating from outer space.

1-64

Of these three explanations, the second has largely been ruled out. The U.S. does not possess the kind of advanced technology witnessed by the pilots. So, that leaves either foreign weapons systems or extraterrestrials. NASA has been quick to point out that there is no evidence UFOs are alien, but they are not dismissing the possibility either. "We
30 have the tools and team who can help us to improve our understanding of the unknown," the organization said. "That's the very definition of what science is. That's what we do." So, are these mysterious objects in the sky developed by human beings in secret projects or are they the first signs of a coming alien invasion? If anyone can find out, NASA can.

Notes

saucer-shaped 円盤のような形
unidentified flying object 未確認飛行物体（UFO）
fascinate 引き付ける，魅了する　**g-force [gravity force]** 重力加速度
tear apart 引き裂く，ばらばらにする　**by no means** 決して～ではない
Department of Defense 国防省　**Congress** 議会　**hypersonic** 極超音速の
witness 目撃する

True / False

次の文が本文の内容と一致する場合は T，一致しない場合は F を記入しましょう。

1. (　　) It is still not clear whether UFOs really exist.
2. (　　) The pilots in 2015 saw a group of UFOs all flying together.
3. (　　) Flying like the 2015 UFOs would have killed an ordinary human pilot.
4. (　　) Two of the possible explanations for UFOs involve human technology.
5. (　　) NASA is sure UFOs are not from outer space.

次の質問に英語で答えましょう。

1. How long were the 2015 UFOs in the sky?

   _____

   _____

2. Why might UFOs be weapons systems developed by Russia or China?

   _____

   _____

3. Which of the three explanations for UFOs seems not to be true?

   _____

   _____

Vocabulary in Context

次の英文の空所に入れるのに正しい語句を下から選びましょう。

1. The evidence shows we must (   ) that explanation.

2. The man's shocked (   ) was heard throughout the building.

3. The (   ) of the aircraft was amazing.

4. What is the exact (   ) of the term?

5. The cameras allow us to (   ) what's happening remotely.

exclamation	agility	observe	rule out	definition

Writing Sentences — Expressing a Purpose

目的を表す表現を学びます。次の英文の (　　) 内の単語を並べ替えて，意味の通る文にしましょう。
大文字の語も小文字で記されています。

1. UFO の正体を知るために調査が開始された。

   An investigation was opened in (UFOs / to / what / understand / order) are.

   (　　　　　　　　　　　　　　　　　　　　　　　　　　　　　　　　　　　　)

2. チームは，実際に起こったことを確認するために録画を見た。

   The team watched the recording so (what / that / could / they / see) really happened.

   (　　　　　　　　　　　　　　　　　　　　　　　　　　　　　　　　　　　　)

3. パイロットは，航空機を操縦する能力を高めるために，厳しい訓練を受けた。

   The pilots trained hard so (their / increase / to / ability / as) to fly the aircraft.

   (　　　　　　　　　　　　　　　　　　　　　　　　　　　　　　　　　　　　)

Listening Summary   1-65

音声を聞いて，次の英文の空所を埋めましょう。

There are many things about [1)]_____, or UFOs, we don't understand, but one thing we do know is that they do exist. In the past two decades, there have been more than 400 sightings by military pilots in the U.S. of objects in the sky whose [2)]_____ exceed all known human technology. [3)]_____ high-level government organizations, including NASA, have concluded that there are three [4)]_____. One is that the objects are weapons developed by foreign powers like China or Russia; another is that they [5)]_____ secret projects within the U.S. military; and the third is that they are extraterrestrial. The second option has [6)]_____, so that leaves either one or three. Both are rather frightening explanations.

A. クラスメートと話し合って，円の中にあるテーマに関係している単語をリストアップしてみましょう。

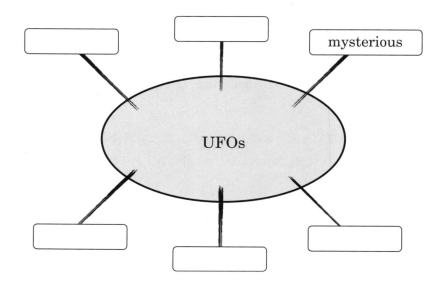

mysterious

UFOs

B. 次の英文を読んで，自分の考えを書きましょう。

1. What do you think is the most likely explanation for UFOs?

2. Do you believe that aliens exist on other planets? Do you think we will ever meet them?

Hard Gardening

Growing Plants on the Moon

植物を栽培するのがとても難しい場所, それは月かもしれません。なぜなら月のダストには, 植物を育てるのに必要な成分がほとんど含まれていないからです。しかし, 人類が太陽系を植民地化したいのであれば, 植物の栽培を実現しなければなりません。科学者がチャレンジした結果, どうなったでしょうか。

Key Vocabulary

次の単語について，その定義を結びつけましょう。

1. colonize   (a) the layer of earth plants grow in

2. solar system   (b) to begin to produce leaves from a seed

3. soil   (c) to send people to live in another country or planet

4. scarce   (d) to copy or simulate

5. mimic   (e) rare or available in only small amounts

6. sprout   (f) to change or adjust

7. alter   (g) the sun and planets including Earth

1-67

Of all the places you might think about creating a garden, the Moon is probably the last one that would come to mind. But if human beings ever want to colonize our solar system, starting with the Moon or perhaps Mars, we will have to learn how to grow food in the inhospitable conditions of space. That's why there was a great deal of scientific
5 interest in a project launched by researchers at the University of Florida which aimed to find out whether plants could grow in soil taken from the Moon.

1-68

There were two huge challenges to the project. The first was that moon soil is extremely scarce on Earth. The only samples available were taken from the Apollo missions in the 1960s and 1970s, over 50 years ago, and there is a lot of demand to use them from
10 scientists working in various fields. The three researchers at the University of Florida were able to gain a total of 12 grams from Apollo 11, Apollo 12, and Apollo 17, dividing them into pots holding one gram each.

1-69

The second challenge was the soil itself. Moon soil is incredibly harsh, consisting of a fine powder of sharp bits of metallic iron and glass forged by space rocks smashing into
15 the surface. It does not contain nitrogen, phosphorus, or any other nutrients that plants need to grow. Simply put, it is a gardener's worst nightmare.

1-70

So, what happened when the researchers planted seeds in it? Anna-Lisa Paul and her colleagues chose thale cress for their experiment, a small plant that is able to grow in a tiny amount of soil. They planted the seeds in 12 pots of moon dust and 16 pots of
20 volcanic material from Earth, a substance often used to mimic moon dust for experiments. Watering them with a soup of nutrients, they waited for the fast-growing cress to sprout.

1-71

It did not take long for success to come. Tiny sprouts appeared in all the pots of moon dust, the very first terrestrial organisms ever to grow in extraterrestrial materials. "That was a moving experience," says Paul, "Amazing. Just amazing." The results, however,
25 were not perfect. None of the moon sample plants grew as well as those in the volcanic

soil. The healthiest were smaller while the least healthy turned purple rather than green, a classic sign of plant stress. The worst ones were from the Apollo 11 soil, which had been on the lunar surface longer than the other samples, exposing it to more sharp bits of glass and iron.

1-72

30 On the whole, the experiment suggested that space gardening is difficult but not impossible. Plants could be genetically altered to make them more suitable for moon soil or the soil itself could be changed by adding nutrients. As a first attempt, however, the Florida team's work was incredibly exciting. Who knows? Perhaps one day we could look up at the Moon and see fields of green.

Notes

inhospitable 荒れ果てた，過酷な **forge** 鍛造する **nitrogen** 窒素 **phosphorus** リン **nutrient** 栄養物 **thale cress** シロイヌナズナ **terrestrial** 地球上の **lunar** 月の **expose to** 〜にさらす

thale cress

True / False

次の文が本文の内容と一致する場合は T，一致しない場合は F を記入しましょう。

1. (　　　　) Only a little soil has been collected from the Moon.

2. (　　　　) Plants require nutrients that are not found on the Moon.

3. (　　　　) The researchers compared moon soil with soil found on Earth.

4. (　　　　) The longer soil has been on the Moon, the better it is for growing food.

5. (　　　　) Growing food on the Moon would seem to be an impossible task.

Understanding Details

次の質問に英語で答えましょう。

1. Why were scientists so interested in the project to grow food in moon soil?

_____

_____

2. How many pots of moon soil did the researchers use?

_____

_____

3. What is the significance of the color purple when it comes to plants?

_____

_____

Vocabulary in Context

次の英文の空所に入れるのに正しい語句を下から選びましょう。

1. We will need to (　　　　　　　) our conclusions in light of this new data.

2. The mineral was so (　　　　　　　) that its value increased every year.

3. The (　　　　　　　) in this area is not rich enough to support many plants.

4. We have still explored only a small part of our (　　　　　　　).

5. To (　　　　　　　) space would be one of humanity's greatest achievements.

colonize	solar system	soil	scarce	alter

Writing Sentences—Gerunds and Infinitives

動名詞と不定詞を学びます。次の英文の（　　）内の単語を並べ替えて，意味の通る文にしましょう。
大文字の語も小文字で記されています。

1. 土壌が少ないので，失敗しないようにしなければならない。

Since the soil is so scarce, we must (mistakes / avoid / try / making / to).

(　　　　　　　　　　　　　　　　　　　　　　　　　　　　　　　　　　　　　)

2. 栄養不足の土壌にもかかわらず，研究者たちは成功した。

The researchers managed (lacking / despite / succeed / to / soil / the) nutrients.

(　　　　　　　　　　　　　　　　　　　　　　　　　　　　　　　　　　　　　)

3. そのまま実験を継続することにした。

We (to / out / continue / decided / carrying) the experiment.

(　　　　　　　　　　　　　　　　　　　　　　　　　　　　　　　　　　　　　)

Listening Summary

 1-73

音声を聞いて，次の英文の空所を埋めましょう。

There can't be many harder places to grow plants than the Moon. But if human beings ever ¹⁾_____ our solar system, growing plants in space is something we will have to do. A team of researchers at the University of Florida ²⁾_____ to discover whether plants can grow in soil taken from the Moon. It was a very challenging task. Moon soil ³⁾_____ on Earth since nobody has set foot there since 1972; moreover, the soil, which consists of metallic iron and glass, contains very few ⁴⁾_____ that plants need to grow. Despite these challenges, however, the team did succeed in their aim, growing terrestrial organisms in ⁵⁾_____ for the very first time. The plants grew up smaller and weaker than normal, indicating the difficulty of the task. However, the researchers ⁶⁾_____ about how to turn the dream of space gardening into reality.

Express your Ideas

A. クラスメートと話し合って，円の中にあるテーマに関係している単語をリストアップしてみ
ましょう。

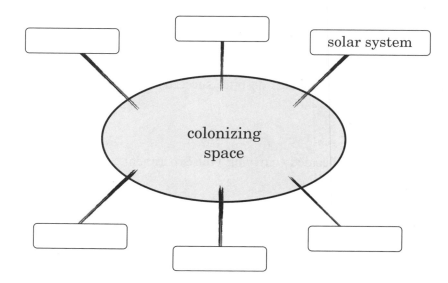

B. 次の英文を読んで，自分の考えを書きましょう。

1. Do you think we should try to colonize the Moon or Mars? Why / why not?

_____

_____

_____

2. What are the biggest challenges to doing so?

_____

_____

_____

UNIT 11

Seeds of Life

Hayabusa's Great Discovery

2018 年，日本の探査機「はやぶさ 2」が「リュウグウ」という小惑星に着陸しました。「はやぶさ」のミッションは，小惑星からサンプルを採取し，地球に持ち帰って分析することでした。「はやぶさ」は何を発見したのでしょうか。そして，なぜそれは重要な発見だったのでしょう。

Key Vocabulary

次の単語について，その定義を結びつけましょう。

1. launch   **(a)** a large rock circling the Sun

2. asteroid   **(b)** exact and accurate

3. orbit   **(c)** a rock that hits the Earth from space

4. generate   **(d)** to produce or create

5. precise   **(e)** to send a spacecraft into the sky

6. accomplish   **(f)** to achieve a goal

7. meteorite   **(g)** to move around a planet or star

1-75

On 3 December 2014, a spacecraft took off from the launch site of the Japan Space Agency (JAXA) in Tanegashima in Kyushu. Hayabusa2 was headed for an asteroid known as Ryugu, which orbits the Sun between Earth and Mars. JAXA aimed to land the spacecraft on the surface of the asteroid in order to collect samples that it would then
5 bring back to Earth for analysis. The mission was generating excitement from scientists all over the world since asteroids like Ryugu are thought to have formed during the earliest stages of our solar system, offering us a view of the past that can't be found in any history book.

1-76

It took four years for Hayabusa to reach Ryugu, and then came the incredibly complex
10 and precise challenge of landing the spacecraft on a small, rotating object traveling at around 100,000 kilometers an hour. Scientists at JAXA held their breath as they guided the craft down, but on 21 September 2018, they successfully deployed two rovers on the surface of the asteroid, followed soon after by a third. A few months later, they landed an impactor designed to break through the surface and collect samples from under the
15 ground.

1-77

After accomplishing its goals, Hayabusa flew back to Earth, arriving home in December 2020. The analysis of the 5.4 grams of dust and rocks it had collected began immediately. One of the first things the researchers found was that the chemical composition of the material was somewhat different from the objects scientists had previously relied on to
20 get an understanding of the distant past: meteorites that had fallen to Earth. It appeared to be more "primitive," that is closer to the material of the early solar system, likely because it had not been changed by Earth's environment. "The Ryugu material is the most primitive material in the solar system we have ever studied," said Hisayoshi Yurimoto, the leader of the chemical analysis team.

1-78

25 Even more exciting was the discovery of 23 types of amino acids in the Ryugu samples. Amino acids are the building blocks of proteins produced by living organisms and,

therefore, a key part of life itself. Scientists had long speculated about how such amino acids had come to exist on Earth. Were they created naturally in Earth's atmosphere by lightning strikes, for example, or did they arrive on a meteorite? The Ryugu samples seem
30 to suggest the latter. As Kensei Kobayashi, an astrobiologist from Yokohama National University, commented: "Scientists have been questioning how organic matter was created or where it came from, and the fact that amino acids were discovered in the sample offers a reason to think that amino acids were brought to Earth from outer space."

 1-79

It is incredible to think that the whole history of life on Earth might have started with a
35 meteorite crashing into our planet. Who knows what other secrets Ryugu holds?

Notes
deploy 配備する, 配置する **rover** 惑星探査機, ローバー
impactor インパクタ **chemical composition** 化学成分, 化学組成
amino acid アミノ酸 **speculate** 推測する **astrobiologist** 宇宙生物学者
organic matter 有機物

True / False

次の文が本文の内容と一致する場合は T, 一致しない場合は F を記入しましょう。

1. (   ) Ryugu is closer to the Sun than the Earth is.

2. (   ) The article mentions four machines that Hayabusa landed on the asteroid.

3. (   ) Hayabusa collected samples from both on and under the surface of Ryugu.

4. (   ) Analysis confirmed that Ryugu formed during the early stages of the solar system.

5. (   ) The Hayabusa project suggests life on Earth began through a lightning strike.

次の質問に英語で答えましょう。

1. About how fast is Ryugu moving through space?

_____

_____

2. Why do meteorites not provide such a "primitive" view of the solar system?

_____

_____

3. What was the most exciting discovery from the Ryugu samples?

_____

_____

Vocabulary in Context

次の英文の空所に入れるのに正しい語句を下から選びましょう。

1. The machine made a very (   ) cut in the metal.

2. Everybody looked up to see a (   ) flash across the sky.

3. The (   ) of Earth around the Sun takes one year.

4. JAXA made a successful (   ) of the new rocket.

5. We managed to (   ) all our goals for the mission.

launch	orbit	precise	accomplish	meteorite

Writing Sentences — Expressing Probabilities

可能性の表現を学びます。次の英文の（　　）内の単語を並べ替えて，意味の通る文にしましょう。大文字の語も小文字で記されています。

1. アミノ酸は，隕石によって地球にもたらされた可能性が高い。

It (amino / likely / were / that / is / acids) brought to Earth by a meteorite.

(　　　　　　　　　　　　　　　　　　　　　　　　　　　　　　　　　　　　　)

2. このサンプルを分析すれば，きっと面白い結果が得られるに違いない。

The analysis of the sample (interesting / sure / bring / some / to / was) results.

(　　　　　　　　　　　　　　　　　　　　　　　　　　　　　　　　　　　　　)

3. ミッションが成功しない可能性もある。

There (that / a / mission / possibility / is / the) will not succeed.

(　　　　　　　　　　　　　　　　　　　　　　　　　　　　　　　　　　　　　)

Listening Summary 1-80

音声を聞いて，次の英文の空所を埋めましょう。

In 2014, a special mission [1)]_____ the Japanese Space Agency, JAXA. Its aim was to land a spacecraft on the surface of an asteroid called Ryugu which [2)]_____ Earth and Mars. The mission was important because asteroids like Ryugu are believed to have formed in the early stages of [3)]_____, giving us a valuable view of this unknown past. Hayabusa2 successfully landed on Ryugu and [4)]_____ of dust and rock that were transported back to Earth. Analysis of the samples showed not only that the asteroid [5)]_____ material from the early solar system but that it contained types of amino acids, which are one of the building blocks of life on Earth. The discovery showed that meteorites might have brought these [6)]_____ to our planet.

A. クラスメートと話し合って，円の中にあるテーマに関係している単語をリストアップしてみましょう。

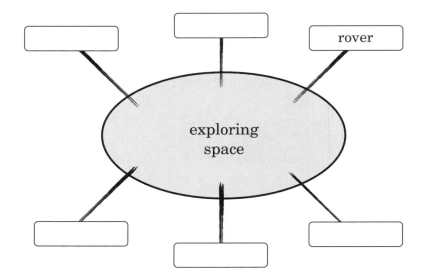

rover

exploring
space

B. 次の英文を読んで，自分の考えを書きましょう。

1. Are you interested in space exploration? What things interest you the most?

_____

_____

_____

2. It costs a lot of money to send spacecraft to space. Do you think it is worth the cost?

_____

_____

_____

UNIT 12

Unlimited Resources

The Prospect of Mining Space

地球上では，水や金属，鉱物などの資源をめぐる競争が激化しています。しかし，もし資源を無限に採掘できるとしたらどうでしょう。理屈の上では，太陽系の衛星や小惑星には，その可能性が秘められています。実際に宇宙で採掘を始める可能性はあるのでしょうか。

Key Vocabulary

次の単語について，その定義を結びつけましょう。

1. resources   (a) making something sound bigger than it really is

2. wealth   (b) useful materials a country has e.g. oil, gas, and minerals

3. estimate   (c) to support something so that it can continue

4. exaggeration   (d) related to the law

5. operation   (e) to guess the size or value

6. legal   (f) controlling a machine or vehicle

7. sustain   (g) a large amount of money

🎧 1-82

One of the many challenges facing the human race today is competition for resources. Our modern societies depend on common substances like water, iron, and oil for energy and consumption and they also require much scarcer materials such as platinum, gold, and so-called "rare earth minerals" for the building of computers, smartphones, and other electronic devices. As demand grows year by year, competition to find new resources will only increase.

🎧 1-83

Is there any way to deal with this problem? For some scientists, the solution lies not on Earth but in space. Within our solar system, there are asteroids and moons that contain mineral wealth far greater than anything we can dream about on our own planet. In one famous example, a 226-kilometer asteroid named 16 Psyche is said to have iron and nickel resources estimated to be worth 10 quintillion dollars, about 100,000 times the size of the world's GDP. Although that is surely an exaggeration, there is no doubt there are incredible riches available for any companies brave enough to take on the challenge of mining in space.

🎧 1-84

How likely is it that they could do so, and where would mining start? Most experts believe the Moon would be the most obvious place to begin. It requires a journey of only several days by rocket and creates communication lags of just a couple of seconds – a delay short enough to allow remote operation of robots from Earth. Moreover, its low gravity means that relatively little energy would be needed to deliver its resources to Earth. The Moon may look like a barren rock, but recent probes have shown that it contains a substantial amount of hidden water ice at the poles. It also appears to have significant deposits of Helium-3, a potential fuel source for nuclear fusion reactors that are expected to be developed over the coming decades.

🎧 1-85

Along with the Moon, there are many asteroids orbiting between Earth and Mars that could be targeted for mining. Although requiring much longer travel times, they are likely to contain large amounts of rare earth minerals that could make the extra cost of reaching them worth it.

1-86

Despite the rewards, however, space mining will hardly be a simple task. As well as the huge cost of launching rockets large enough to carry the equipment necessary for mining, there are the challenges of carrying out the work itself in environments of no air, low gravity, and extreme temperatures. There are also legal issues to solve. How do we decide who owns the rights to mine the Moon, for example?

1-87

Interestingly, several countries, including the United States, China, Russia, and Japan, are already working on laws that would make it possible for private companies to claim a right to resources in space. It may be a long time before the first mine opens, but one day we may have ships flying to and from space, carrying the minerals we need to sustain our lives on Earth.

Notes

substance 物質　**platinum** プラチナ, 白金　**rare earth mineral** 希土類鉱物
nickel ニッケル　**GDP (Gross Domestic Product)** 国民総生産
lag 遅れ, 時間差　**barren** 不毛な　**probe** 探査, 調査　**deposit** 鉱床
potential 可能性のある　**nuclear fusion reactor** 核融合炉

True / False

次の文が本文の内容と一致する場合は T, 一致しない場合は F を記入しましょう。

1. (　　) There is competition for both common and scarce resources.

2. (　　) 16 Psyche probably does not really have $10 quintillion worth of resources.

3. (　　) It is very hard to operate robots on the Moon remotely because of the distance from Earth.

4. (　　) It would not be worth the cost of traveling all the way to asteroids for mining.

5. (　　) We would have to overcome legal and technological challenges to mine in space.

次の質問に英語で答えましょう。

1. What do we call the minerals needed for building electronic devices?

   _____

   _____

2. What would Helium-3 be used for potentially?

   _____

   _____

3. What is the purpose of the laws being worked on in the United States and other countries?

   _____

   _____

Vocabulary in Context

次の英文の空所に入れるのに正しい語句を下から選びましょう。

1. We need many resources in order to (　　　　　　) our modern lifestyles.

2. It is no (　　　　　) to say that global warming affects everyone on Earth.

3. We have so much (　　　　　) but it is not shared equally.

4. The (　　　　　) of these machines requires a lot of training.

5. It is hard to (　　　　　) the true value of these resources.

wealth	estimate	exaggeration	operation	sustain

Writing Sentences — Giving Examples

例を挙げる表現を学びます。次の英文の（　　）内の単語を並べ替えて，意味の通る文にしましょう。
大文字の語も小文字で記されています。

1. 電子機器に使用される鉱物など，現代社会には多くの資源が使用されている。

Many resources are used in modern society, (as / minerals / in / the / such / used)
electronic devices.

(　　　　　　　　　　　　　　　　　　　　　　　　　　　　　　　　　　　　　　)

2. 月は地球から近いということも含め，採掘にはいくつかの利点がある。

The Moon offers several advantages for mining, (fact / that / the / it / including) is so
close to Earth.

(　　　　　　　　　　　　　　　　　　　　　　　　　　　　　　　　　　　　　　)

3. 日本のような国は，未来を維持するために新たな資源を見つける必要がある。

(to / like / will / countries / need / Japan) find new resources to sustain its future.

(　　　　　　　　　　　　　　　　　　　　　　　　　　　　　　　　　　　　　　)

Listening Summary

 1-88

音声を聞いて，次の英文の空所を埋めましょう。

Our modern lifestyles create a ¹⁾_____ for resources such as
water, oil, metals, and minerals. Since there is only a limited supply, competition for
these resources will increase. What can we do about it? One solution is to look for new
resources ²⁾_____ but in space. Within our solar system,
there are ³⁾_____ that contain incredible deposits of metal
and minerals. Is it possible we could get them? Experts say the Moon is the first place
we could target since it is close enough to allow the ⁴⁾_____
of robots from our planet. But the real wealth lies in asteroids further away. Mining
them would require us to overcome ⁵⁾_____. There are
technical issues of working in such ⁶⁾_____ and legal issues
about ownership of rights. But the fact that countries are developing new space laws
shows they are serious about taking on these challenges.

A. クラスメートと話し合って，円の中にあるテーマに関係している単語をリストアップしてみましょう。

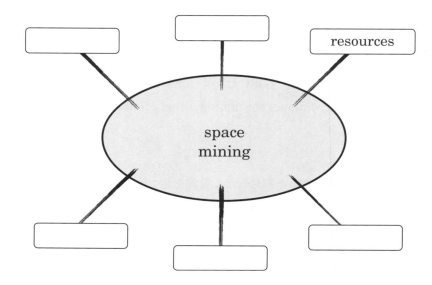

B. 次の英文を読んで，自分の考えを書きましょう。

1. Does the world use too many resources now? How can we reduce our use of them?

_____

_____

_____

2. Do you think that space mining will become a reality?

_____

_____

_____

UNIT 13

An Itchy Problem

The Science of Mosquito Bites

刺されたと感じるときにはもう，蚊の姿はありません。蚊がなぜ私たちを刺すのか，また，どのようにして刺すのかについては，よく知られています。しかし，なぜ蚊に狙われる人とそうでない人がいるのか，という理由は分かっていません。しかし，科学はようやくその答えを導き出そうとしています。

Key Vocabulary

次の単語について，その定義を結びつけましょう。

1. mosquito   **(a)** the liquid made inside your mouth

2. saliva   **(b)** having a baby inside you

3. attract   **(c)** to make someone come to you

4. detect   **(d)** one of several things that cause an event

5. pregnant   **(e)** to discover from a distance

6. odor   **(f)** a smell, often bad

7. factor   **(g)** a small flying insect that sucks your blood

CD 2-02

When it comes to summer in Japan, it is the heat and humidity that tend to bother people the most. But there is another common irritant too: the little mosquito. Mosquitoes bite us because human and animal blood happens to contain the nutrients they need to develop their eggs. When they land on us, female mosquitoes (male mosquitoes don't
5 bite) inject six tiny needles into our skin. These needles are used to drill through the skin, hold the hole open, suck out the blood, and inject saliva into the blood vessel. The saliva acts as an anticoagulant to keep the blood flowing, and it is an allergic reaction to this substance that causes the itchy spot we all know and hate.

CD 2-03

So far, so disgusting. But while the biology of a mosquito bite is well understood by
10 scientists, there is one question that has puzzled them for many years: Why do mosquitoes bite some people more than others? We know that certain aspects of human biology attract mosquitoes. Carbon dioxide is usually the first chemical the insects detect – from as far as 50 meters away – and since larger creatures breathe out more CO_2, this means that men tend to get bitten more than women, adults more than children, and pregnant
15 women more than non-pregnant women. They are also drawn by heat, sweat, body odor, and, some studies suggest, color. Dark colors like black and red appear to be more visible to mosquitoes than light ones.

CD 2-04

But this still doesn't explain why two people of similar size can get bitten to very different degrees. Is there another factor involved? Recently, a team from Rockefeller University in
20 the U.S. published a study that suggested some answers. The researchers asked 64 volunteers to wear nylon stockings on their arms for six hours a day over multiple days. At the end of the experiment, the team placed the stockings into a tank and released mosquitoes inside to observe which stocking drew more insects. Shockingly, some stockings attracted 100 times more mosquitoes than others.

CD 2-05

25 An examination of the chemicals on the skin of each participant revealed that those attractive to mosquitoes had much higher rates of carboxylic acid than those who

weren't. Carboxylic acid is a natural substance that keeps our skin moisturized. While it is not smelly in itself, the bacteria that feed on it create an odor that appears to be easy for mosquitoes to detect. The bad news is there is nothing we can do to reduce the production of carboxylic acid in our bodies. However, it might be possible to develop skin products or insect repellents that hide the odor from mosquitoes. A summer without mosquito bites would be just a little easier to bear.

Notes **irritant** イライラさせるもの **drill through** 穴をあける **blood vessel** 血管
anticoagulant 抗凝固剤 **allergic reaction** アレルギー反応
drew draw（引き寄せる）の過去形 **carboxylic acid** カルボン酸
keep moisturized うるおいを保つ

True / False

次の文が本文の内容と一致する場合は T，一致しない場合は F を記入しましょう。

1. (　　) Human blood contains nutrients that male mosquitoes need for food.

2. (　　) The itchy spot left by a mosquito bite is caused by saliva.

3. (　　) The more carbon dioxide you emit, the more likely you are to be bitten by a mosquito.

4. (　　) In the Rockefeller University experiment, participants had to put their arms into a tank.

5. (　　) Carboxylic acid is a harmful and smelly chemical.

次の質問に英語で答えましょう。

1. What is the purpose of the saliva injected into our blood vessels by mosquitoes?

_____

_____

2. Name five factors that allow mosquitoes to detect us, according to the second paragraph.

_____

_____

3. What creates the odor from carboxylic acid that mosquitoes can detect?

_____

_____

Vocabulary in Context

次の英文の空所に入れるのに正しい語句を下から選びましょう。

1. The researchers discovered another (   ) causing the phenomenon.

2. The new fighter plane is impossible for radar to (   ).

3. The (   ) emitted by the chemical was terrible.

4. It was not obvious immediately that the woman was (   ).

5. We can (   ) new customers with this product.

attract	detect	pregnant	odor	factor

Writing Sentences — Giving Advice

アドバイスする表現を学びます。次の英文の (　) 内の単語を並べ替えて，意味の通る文にしましょう。大文字の語も小文字で記されています。

1. 外に出る予定がある場合は，虫除けスプレーを使用するべきだ。

   You (to / insect / use / repellent / ought / if) you plan to go outside.

   (　　　　　　　　　　　　　　　　　　　　　　　　　　　　)

2. 夜間は窓を閉めた方がいい。

   (would / to / better / be / close / it) the windows during the evening.

   (　　　　　　　　　　　　　　　　　　　　　　　　　　　　)

3. 彼は皮膚の痒い部分を引っ掻かない方がよかった。

   He (the / scratched / shouldn't / itchy / have) spot on his skin.

   (　　　　　　　　　　　　　　　　　　　　　　　　　　　　)

Listening Summary

CD 2-06

音声を聞いて，次の英文の空所を埋めましょう。

Mosquitoes bite humans and animals because blood 1)_____
they need for their eggs. When they bite us, they 2)_____
through our skin to keep the blood flowing. This substance causes an allergic reaction,
leaving us with an itchy spot. Mosquitoes usually detect us first by the
3)_____ we breathe out, meaning that larger creatures tend
to be bitten more than smaller ones. They can also detect heat, sweat, body odor, and,
perhaps, dark colors. But even accounting for size, it appears some individuals are
4)_____ to mosquitoes than others. Why is that? A recent
study suggested that a chemical called carboxylic acid might be responsible. Carboxylic
acid is a 5)_____ that keeps our skin moisturized, and some
people produce more of it than others. Researchers 6)_____
might help us to find ways to keep these biting insects away.

A. クラスメートと話し合って，円の中にあるテーマに関係している単語をリストアップしてみましょう。

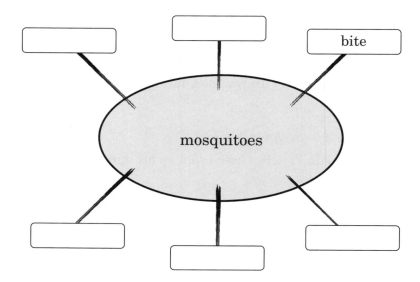

B. 次の英文を読んで，自分の考えを書きましょう。

1. Do you often get bitten by mosquitoes? Do you know anyone who doesn't get bitten often?

_____

_____

_____

2. Since mosquitoes carry serious diseases like malaria, some people say we should try to eradicate the insects from Earth completely. What do you think about this idea?

_____

_____

_____

Goodbye Diets?

The Exercise Pill

運動は，体重を減らすために重要な要素だと思われています。しかし，時にそれが逆効果になることもあるのです。なぜでしょうか。最近，科学者たちはその答えとなるような研究を行いました。この研究による発見は，ダイエット中の人が努力せずに体重を減らすのに役立つかもしれません。

Key Vocabulary

次の単語について，その定義を結びつけましょう。

1. benefit   **(a)** to control or stop certain feelings

2. complex   **(b)** the feeling of wanting to eat

3. suppress   **(c)** difficult to understand, complicated

4. molecule   **(d)** amount or number of something

5. quantity   **(e)** to put a drug into a person with a needle

6. appetite   **(f)** the smallest unit of a substance consisting of one or more atoms

7. inject   **(g)** something that helps you

🎵 CD 2-08

Unless you're one of those lucky people who can eat as much as they want without any impact on their waistline, the chances are that at some point in your life, you're going to think about trying to lose weight. When we think of losing weight, we usually imagine two things: going on a diet and exercising. But while exercising has many clear benefits,
5   including improving our general physical and mental health, its relationship to cutting the kilos is more complex. Studies show that it can have either a positive or a negative effect. Why is that?

🎵 CD 2-09

Fundamentally, if we want to lose weight, we have to burn more calories than we consume. Exercising is one way to burn calories quickly, so there is no doubt it can be a
10   powerful weapon if done effectively. The problem is that many people find that exercising increases their feelings of hunger. If you go for a five-kilometer run and then immediately stuff a donut in your mouth, you're not going to do much good.

🎵 CD 2-10

So, is there a way to suppress that urge to eat after exercise? A team of scientists recently created an interesting experiment to find out. They set a group of mice to run on tiny
15   treadmills at increasing speeds until they were tired out. Then they tested the blood of the mice to see if there were any differences before and after the exercise. One difference stood out: a molecule related to lactate, the chemical produced during exercise that causes a burning sensation in our muscles. Calling this new molecule lac-phe, the scientists found that it appeared in greater quantities the more intensely the mice
20   exercised.

🎵 CD 2-11

The researchers then wondered whether lac-phe might have any connection with appetite. They injected obese mice with the molecule before offering them their usual large meal. To the team's surprise, the mice ate 30 percent less than usual. The researchers then turned back to exercise. Breeding a group of mice to produce less lac-phe, they had
25   them exercise on treadmills as before. This time, the mice ate 25 percent more food, gaining weight as a result. Lac-phe, it seems, is a key link between exercise and hunger.

2-12

So, what does this mean for humans hoping to lose weight? For a start, lac-phe is only produced in large quantities after intense exercise. Cycling for an hour at a moderate pace, for example, will generate little, while sprinting at full speed for a short time will
30 produce more. "What the data says is that intensity matters," says Dr. Long, the lead scientist in the study. But lac-phe might also hold the key to the ultimate dream for dieters: a drug that removes the temptation to eat. Could a little pill stop you feeling hungry? Now, that would make everyone feel lucky.

> **Notes** | **waistline** ウエストライン，胴回り　**stuff in your mouth** 詰め込む，口に入れる
> **urge to eat** 食べたいという衝動　**lactate** 乳酸塩，ラクテート　**obese** 肥満体の
> **breed** 繁殖させる　**ultimate** 究極の　**temptation** 誘惑

True / False

次の文が本文の内容と一致する場合は T，一致しない場合は F を記入しましょう。

1. (　　) Exercise is not always the most effective way to lose weight.

2. (　　) If we consume more calories than we burn, we will not lose weight.

3. (　　) Researchers found a new molecule in the blood of the mice before they exercised.

4. (　　) Mice injected with lac-phe ate less than usual.

5. (　　) The more intensely you exercise, the less likely you are to feel hungry afterwards.

次の質問に英語で答えましょう。

1. How did the scientists make the mice tired?

_____

_____

2. Why did one group of mice eat 25 percent more food than usual?

_____

_____

3. What would be the dream for people who want to lose weight, according to the article?

_____

_____

Vocabulary in Context

次の英文の空所に入れるのに正しい語句を下から選びましょう。

1. Having eaten a big lunch, I didn't have much (   ) for dinner.

2. Unfortunately, we did not gain any (   ) from participating in the project.

3. The problem was so (   ) that none of the scientists could solve it.

4. The company discovered a huge (   ) of oil in the desert.

5. This drug should (   ) the main effects of the disease.

benefit	complex	suppress	quantity	appetite

Writing Sentences —Verbs with Prepositions

動詞＋前置詞を学びます。次の英文の（　　）内の単語を並べ替えて，意味の通る文にしましょう。
大文字の語も小文字で記されています。

1. チームは，運動とダイエットに関する研究に取り組んできた。

The team has been (exercise / study / on / about / a / working) and diets.

(   )

2. この研究は，運動が食欲を増進させる理由を解明することを目的としたものである。

The study (discovering / why / at / aimed / is) exercise can stimulate the appetite.

(   )

3. 食欲が増すと，運動しても体重が減らないことがある。

Increased appetite (from / us / losing / can / prevent / weight) after we exercise.

(   )

Listening Summary

CD 2-13

音声を聞いて，次の英文の空所を埋めましょう。

Exercise is usually seen as an important part of [1]_____,
but actually it sometimes has the opposite effect. The reason is that exercise can
stimulate the appetite, tempting us to eat when we are done. Scientists have long been
interested in why [2]_____ occurs. Recently, a team of
researchers began to uncover some answers. They tested the blood of mice after they
had exercised and discovered a [3]_____ related to lactate,
which they called lac-phe. When [4]_____ lac-phe into another
group of mice, the animals ate 30 percent less food than usual. And when mice were
bred to produce less lac-phe, they ate 25 percent more. Lac-phe is mainly produced
after intense [5]_____, so it is important to exercise hard if
we want to make use of its effects. But one day, could it be used to produce a pill that
makes us feel [6]_____?

Express your Ideas

A. クラスメートと話し合って，円の中にあるテーマに関係している単語をリストアップしてみましょう。

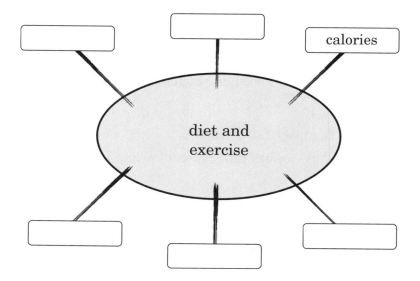

B. 次の英文を読んで，自分の考えを書きましょう。

1. If you wanted to lose weight, do you think it would be easy or difficult? Why?

_____

_____

_____

2. Do you exercise? What kind of exercise do you do and why do you do it?

_____

_____

_____

Regeneration King

The Incredible Power of the Liver

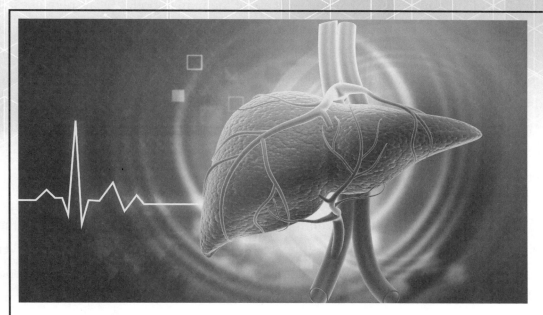

もし，あなたの肝臓に年齢を聞くことができたら，意外な答えが返ってくるかもしれません。なぜなら，肝臓は人体の他の臓器にはない素晴らしい力を持っているからです。その力とは何でしょうか。また，なぜ肝臓はその力を必要としているのでしょうか。

Key Vocabulary

次の単語について，その定義を結びつけましょう。

1. equator   **(a)** to gradually take something in

2. organ   **(b)** very important or necessary

3. absorb   **(c)** to become smaller or less

4. vital   **(d)** part of the body like the heart or liver

5. determine   **(e)** to decide or find out

6. decline   **(f)** protected from disease or damage

7. immune   **(g)** the imaginary line around the center of Earth

2-15

Would you like to hear some amazing facts about the human body? Okay, here goes. If you stretched out all the body's blood vessels, they would have a total length of almost 100,000 kilometers, enough to circle Earth's equator two and a half times. Here's another one. The largest organ in the body is the skin, and each day we shed over 30,000 dead
5　skin cells. In fact, the entire surface of our skin is replaced every month. Third interesting fact. You are about one centimeter taller in the morning than when you go to bed because Earth's gravity compresses your spine during the day. And a final one. In an average lifetime, a person will spend over a year on the toilet. A year.

2-16

So, what does this all have to do with the liver? Well, not much, except that, of all the
10　amazing things about the human body, the liver is perhaps the most incredible. The liver is part of the body's digestive system and it has three main functions: to clean your blood and remove harmful toxins; to produce an important digestive juice that helps the body absorb fat; and to break down carbohydrates into a type of sugar called glucose, which is the main source of fuel for our cells. What makes the liver special, however, is not the
15　vital functions it performs but its age. For no matter how old you are, the liver in your body is only around three years of age.

2-17

This amazing fact was not discovered until 2022 when a team of scientists in Germany used a kind of radiocarbon dating to determine the age of livers taken from the bodies of people who died between age 20 and 84. The researchers found that, regardless of the
20　age of the person, the liver was never more than three years old. The reason for this is that the liver has the power to regenerate itself in order to repair the damage it picks up from its role of taking poisons from the blood. While the organ's regenerative power had been known about, scientists had always assumed that it declined with age. The German study proved this was not the case. "No matter if you are 20 or 84, your liver stays on
25　average just under three years old," the lead researcher, Dr. Olaf Bergmann, said.

CD 2-18

At the moment, it doesn't seem that this magic ability can be transferred to other vital organs, like the heart and the kidneys, to keep them forever young. Nor does it make our liver completely immune from damage: chronic liver disease can block its regenerative power. However, it does offer some consolation to us as we get older. Our skin may
30 wrinkle and our muscles start to ache, but at least our liver is as young as it ever was.

shed 排出する, 脱皮する   **compress** 圧迫する   **spine** 背骨, 脊椎   **toxin** 毒素
break down 分解する   **carbohydrate** 炭水化物   **glucose** グルコース
radiocarbon dating 放射性炭素年代測定法   **regenerative power** 再生能力
chronic 慢性的な   **consolation** 慰め   **wrinkle** しわができる

True / False

次の文が本文の内容と一致する場合は T, 一致しない場合は F を記入しましょう。

1. (   ) The liver is the largest organ in the human body.

2. (   ) We are not the same height when we go to bed as when we get up.

3. (   ) One of the liver's jobs is to clean poisons from our blood.

4. (   ) The liver's power to regenerate itself slowly declines as we get older.

5. (   ) Scientists believe they could use the liver's power on other human organs.

Understanding Details

次の質問に英語で答えましょう。

1. Calculating from the information in the article, about how many kilometers is it around the equator?

   _____

   _____

2. What is the importance of glucose according to the article?

   _____

   _____

3. Why is it important for the liver to be able to repair itself?

   _____

   _____

Vocabulary in Context

次の英文の空所に入れるのに正しい語句を下から選びましょう。

1. The liver is a very important (   ) in the body.

2. The astronomers tried to (   ) the exact size of the planet.

3. This disease weakens the body's (   ) system.

4. The country is located on the (   ) so it is hot all year round.

5. We should try to (   ) all the information we can from the lecture.

---

equator	organ	absorb	determine	immune

Writing Sentences—Expressions with Numbers

数字を含む表現を学びます。次の英文の（　）内の単語を並べ替えて，意味の通る文にしましょう。
大文字の語も小文字で記されています。

1. 血管の長さは 10 万キロメートルにも及ぶ。

   Blood vessels are as (long / 100,000 / as / kilometers / many).

   (　　　　　　　　　　　　　　　　　　　　　　　　　　　　)

2. 私たちは 1 日に 3 万個もの角質を排出している。

   Every day we shed (skin / than / no / 30,000 / fewer) cells.

   (　　　　　　　　　　　　　　　　　　　　　　　　　　　　)

3. 実年齢に関係なく，肝臓は 3 歳以上にはならない。

   No matter our actual age, our liver is (than / years / more / three / never) old.

   (　　　　　　　　　　　　　　　　　　　　　　　　　　　　)

Listening Summary

🔊 2-19

音声を聞いて，次の英文の空所を埋めましょう。

There are many amazing things about the human body. Did you know, for example, that our 1)_____ are so long that if we stretched them out, they would circle the equator two and a half times? Perhaps the most impressive of all the 2)_____ is the liver. The liver provides 3)_____ of taking toxins from our blood, as well as other important roles related to digestion. But cleaning out poisons is dangerous work, and for that reason the liver has evolved an ability 4)_____ constantly. This regenerative power means that the organ is never more than three years old. 5)_____ old the rest of our body becomes, the liver always stays the same age. It would be wonderful if all our organs had this 6)_____, but unfortunately that is not the case. Nevertheless, the liver's magical power is one more amazing thing about the human body.

Express your Ideas

A. クラスメートと話し合って，円の中にあるテーマに関係している単語をリストアップしてみましょう。

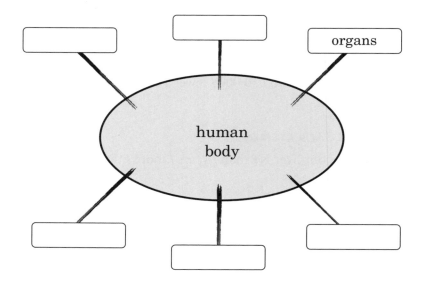

B. 次の英文を読んで，自分の考えを書きましょう。

1. Do you try to look after your body, such as with the food you eat or exercise you take?

_____

_____

_____

2. Have you ever thought you would like to be a doctor? Why / why not?

_____

_____

_____

UNIT 16

Straight to Target

Robots That Swim in the Blood

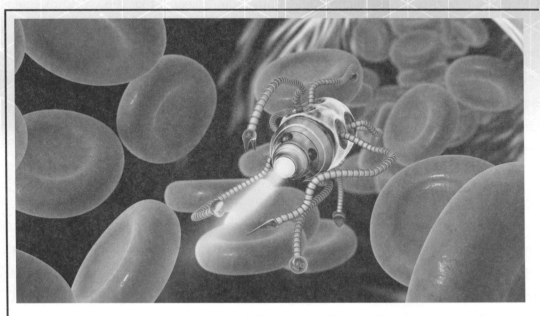

SF作家は，小さな医療ロボットが血液中を泳いで，体の傷ついた部分を的確に治療する世界を長い間想像してきました。今，この技術は少しずつ現実のものになりつつあります。このような未来を実現するためには，どのような課題があるのでしょうか。

Key Vocabulary

次の単語について，その定義を結びつけましょう。

1. miniature
2. overcome
3. adapt
4. fluid
5. constant
6. principle
7. manufacture

(a) a liquid
(b) not changing, happening all the time
(c) extremely small
(d) making or producing something
(e) to change to fit a new situation
(f) a basic idea or rule
(g) to deal with or solve a problem

2-21

With every report of a new technological advance, it seems that the world of science fiction is getting a step closer. The latest leap toward the future came with an announcement that researchers in Switzerland had invented a miniature robot with the ability to swim through the blood to deliver drugs to the exact part of the body they are
5 needed for. The study, published in the journal *Science Advances*, explained how the team had managed to overcome some of the major challenges involved in achieving such a complex objective.

2-22

The most difficult challenge was how to create a soft robot that could adapt to all the different kinds of blood vessels in the human body. Blood vessels are not all the same.
10 Some are wider or narrower than others and they carry fluids of various levels of density, which move at different speeds. To design a machine able to travel at a constant speed through many different conditions, the researchers turned to a surprisingly old kind of human technology: origami. Using the principles of the ancient Japanese art of paper folding, they programmed the robot to change its shape according to the characteristics
15 of the fluid it was moving through. By folding itself into different positions, the machine could maintain its speed and direction in any situation it encountered.

2-23

"Nature has evolved many microorganisms that change shape as their environmental conditions change," said Bradley Nelson, a member of the research team. "This basic principle inspired our micro-robot design."

2-24

20 The second challenge the researchers faced was how to operate the robot once it was inside the body. To deal with this problem, they placed magnetic particles inside the machine to allow it to be controlled via an electromagnetic field. Thanks to this idea, there was no need to use complicated sensors that would have added cost to the manufacture of the robots. Indeed, one of the most attractive features of the micro-robots
25 is how cheap they are to produce.

2-25

The Swiss team is not the only group of scientists working on robots that can travel through the human body. At Hokkaido University in Japan, a robot has been developed that can bend its body to "swim" through fluids like a fish moving in water. Like the Swiss version, this swimming motion allows the robot, which is made from biological
30 molecules, to move through fluids of various levels of density. The swimming speed is relatively fast, at 15 microns per second. On a human scale, this is about 500 meters per hour.

2-26

The actual day when human beings have micro-robots swimming through their blood vessels is not here yet. However, the dreams of science fiction may not be so far away.

Notes

density 密度, 濃度　**microorganism** 微生物　**magnetic particle** 磁性粒子
electromagnetic field 電磁場　**micron** ミクロン (1メートルの100万分の1)

True / False

次の文が本文の内容と一致する場合はT, 一致しない場合はFを記入しましょう。

1. (　　　) The study from Switzerland has already been announced in a journal.

2. (　　　) The miniature robot is only able to travel through one kind of blood vessel.

3. (　　　) The principles of origami were used to decrease the size of the robot.

4. (　　　) The researchers found a cheap way to control the robot inside the body.

5. (　　　) The Hokkaido robot can swim like a fish.

・・

次の質問に英語で答えましょう。

1. What is the purpose of making a robot that can swim through the blood?

_____

_____

2. How many challenges of making the robot are discussed by the article in detail?

_____

_____

3. What is the Hokkaido robot made from?

_____

_____

Vocabulary in Context

・・

次の英文の空所に入れるのに正しい語句を下から選びましょう。

1. Can you explain the (　　　　　　) the new design is based on?

2. We have to (　　　　　) these difficulties if we want to succeed.

3. The employees got tired of their manager's (　　　　　　) demands to work overtime.

4. The (　　　　　) of the product was delayed due to a faulty machine part.

5. It is important to (　　　　　) to a new environment.

overcome	adapt	constant	principle	manufacture

Writing Sentences—Expressing Necessity

必要性を表す表現を学びます。次の英文の（　）内の単語を並べ替えて，意味の通る文にしましょう。大文字の語も小文字で記されています。

1. 研究者は，ロボットが一定の速度で移動できることを確認しなければならなかった。

The researchers (had / robot / to / sure / make / the) could move at a constant speed.

(　　　　　　　　　　　　　　　　　　　　　　　　　　　　　　　)

2. ロボットは，さまざまな種類の血管の中を移動することが必要である。

(necessary / robot / for / the / to / is / it) travel through different kinds of blood vessels.

(　　　　　　　　　　　　　　　　　　　　　　　　　　　　　　　)

3. 成功するためには，これらの課題を克服するしかない。

(is / to / there / choice / no / but) overcome these challenges in order to succeed.

(　　　　　　　　　　　　　　　　　　　　　　　　　　　　　　　)

Listening Summary 🄲🄳 2-27

音声を聞いて，次の英文の空所を埋めましょう。

A research team in Switzerland recently announced the invention of
1)_____ that can swim through the blood to deliver drugs directly to any part of the body they are needed for. In order to do so, they
2)_____ two main challenges. The first was to create a robot that could travel through all the types of blood vessels in the body at
3)_____, adapting to fluids of different density. The researchers achieved this by programming the robot 4)_____ into various positions using the principles of origami. The second challenge was finding a way to control it 5)_____ expensive sensors. This was done by placing magnetic particles inside the machine 6)_____ to be moved by a magnetic field. Around the world, various scientific teams, including in Japan, are working on similar micro-robots. It seems like science fiction stories are starting to come true.

Express your Ideas

A. クラスメートと話し合って，円の中にあるテーマに関係している単語をリストアップしてみましょう。

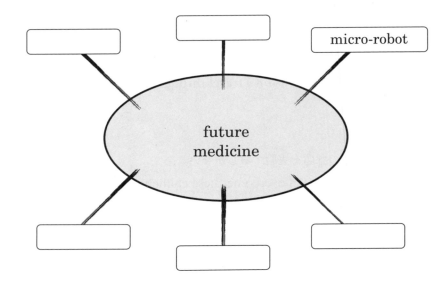

B. 次の英文を読んで，自分の考えを書きましょう。

1. In what ways do you think medicine will advance in the future?

_____

_____

_____

2. Some people think that in the future medicine will advance so far human beings will be able to live forever. Do you think this will be a good thing?

_____

_____

_____

Closer to Humans

Developing Robots with Skin

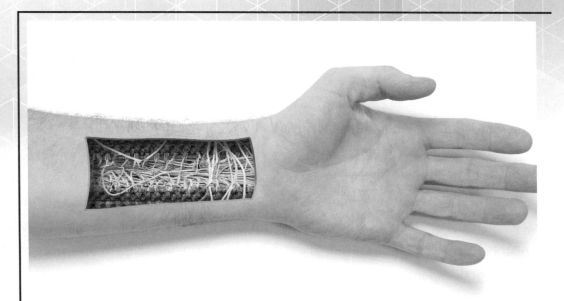

介護施設では，まるで人間のように入居者と接することができるロボットが使われています。しかし，現在のロボットは，本物の人間にはあまり似ていません。そんな中，日本の研究者がその問題を解決するべく画期的な発明をしました。いったいどんな発明なのでしょうか。

次の単語について，その定義を結びつけましょう。

1. breakthrough   **(a)** feature or characteristic of something

2. quality   **(b)** a person you work with

3. time-consuming   **(c)** a liquid in which a substance is dissolved

4. component   **(d)** taking a lot of time to do

5. solution   **(e)** a piece of cloth tied around a wound

6. bandage   **(f)** a part of which something is made

7. colleague   **(g)** a large and sudden advance

2-29

What is the ultimate goal of makers of humanoid robots today? You might say it is to create a machine that looks, acts, and communicates just like a real human being. At the moment, we are still a long way from achieving any of those three things. However, scientists in Japan have recently made a breakthrough that makes at least the first of them
5 a realistic prospect. A team from the University of Tokyo have announced a new way of creating robot skin that looks and feels remarkably like the real thing.

2-30

Manufacturers of androids today use silicone to mimic the appearance of human skin. However, silicone is not able to reproduce the delicate textures and qualities that characterize real tissue. It is also difficult to get silicone to conform to the dynamic curves
10 of human body parts, requiring a skilled artisan who can cut and shape it one piece at a time. This is both expensive and time-consuming.

2-31

The skin created by the Japanese team does not use silicone but components of living human tissue: a liquid solution of collagen and skin cells. Instead of having to cut and shape the skin, the researchers were able to simply place the robot into the solution,
15 which moved into the correct form. Although so far they have done so only with a single robot finger, the results have been very encouraging: "The finger looks slightly sweaty," says Professor Shoji Takeuchi, the head of the study. "Since the finger is driven by an electric motor, it is also interesting to hear the clicking sounds of the motor in harmony with a finger that looks just like a real one."

2-32

20 The new skin offers several advantages over its silicone rival. Not only does it look and feel like living tissue, it is strong enough to bend naturally with the movement of the finger, thick enough not to tear when pinched, and resistant to water. It can even heal itself with the help of a collagen bandage that is gradually absorbed to form new tissue.

2-33

The skin is another step toward producing robots that look human enough for us to be
25 able to feel a connection with them as we interact, an important quality in the
environments these products are likely to be used, such as care homes and hospitals.
However, for Takeuchi and his colleagues, the job is not yet done. They point out that
human skin is more than just a simple cover for our bodies. It has hairs, sweat glands,
and sensors that feel temperature and pain, characteristics that the team are planning to
30 add over the coming years. As Takeuchi says, "This work is just the first step toward
creating robots covered with living skin."

> **Notes**
>
> **humanoid robot** 人型ロボット **prospect** 見込み, 可能性
> **characterize** 特徴づける **tissue** 組織
> **conform to** フィットさせる, 一致させる **artisan** 職人 **harmony** 調和
> **pinch** つまむ, つねる **sweat gland** 汗腺

True / False

次の文が本文の内容と一致する場合は T, 一致しない場合は F を記入しましょう。

1. (　　　) We are close to creating robots that act and communicate like human beings.

2. (　　　) Silicone cannot really reproduce the details of human skin.

3. (　　　) The University of Tokyo skin is made up of biological components.

4. (　　　) The new skin does not tear as easily as silicone skin.

5. (　　　) Takeuchi and his team feel their skin is almost perfect now.

次の質問に英語で答えましょう。

1. Why is an artisan needed to cut and shape silicone skin?

_____

_____

2. What do the researchers use to heal damage to the new skin?

_____

_____

3. What characteristics are the team planning to add to the skin from now on?

_____

_____

Vocabulary in Context

次の英文の空所に入れるのに正しい語句を下から選びましょう。

1. The team made an important (   ) in their research.

2. I will have to ask my (   ) if she agrees with my conclusion.

3. The liquid is a (   ) of salt and water.

4. I cannot believe how (   ) the process is.

5. We had to replace a faulty (   ) in the device.

breakthrough   time-consuming   component   solution   colleague

Writing Sentences — Expressing Expectations

期待・予想を表す表現を学びます。次の英文の（　）内の単語を並べ替えて，意味の通る文にしましょう。
大文字の語も小文字で記されています。

1. 科学者たちは，ロボット技術の急速な発展を期待している。

Scientists (move / to / technology / expect / forward / robot) quickly.

(　　　　　　　　　　　　　　　　　　　　　　　　　　　　　　　　　　　　)

2. このプロジェクトは，来年には終了する予定だ。

This project (to / supposed / finished / is / be) next year.

(　　　　　　　　　　　　　　　　　　　　　　　　　　　　　　　　　　　　)

3. この発明は，ロボットに対する私たちの理解を前進させるきっかけになるはずだ。

The invention (an / should / in / advance / provide) our understanding of robots.

(　　　　　　　　　　　　　　　　　　　　　　　　　　　　　　　　　　　　)

Listening Summary

🎧 2-34

音声を聞いて，次の英文の空所を埋めましょう。

We are still a long way from [1]_____ that look, act, and communicate as if they were real human beings. Researchers in Japan, however, have recently made a breakthrough that could help to make the first of those things [2]_____: living skin. Current robot skin is made from silicone, but there are disadvantages [3]_____ how realistic it looks and how difficult it is to fit to a humanoid robot. The new skin solves these problems by being made [4]_____ of components of living human tissue. As well as looking and feeling like the real thing, the skin is strong enough to [5]_____ and thick enough not to tear easily. It can even heal itself by using a collagen bandage. While there are still [6]_____ of real human skin that the new product lacks, it is a first step toward making robots that look just like us.

Express your Ideas

A. クラスメートと話し合って，円の中にあるテーマに関係している単語をリストアップしてみましょう。

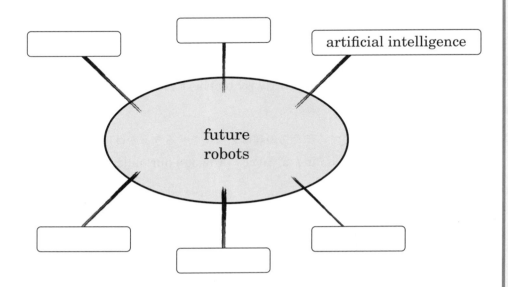

artificial intelligence

future
robots

B. 次の英文を読んで，自分の考えを書きましょう。

1. Imagine the world in 100 years' time. What will robots be able to do?

_____

_____

_____

2. Do you think we should create robots that look, act, and communicate like human beings?

_____

_____

_____

A New Solution

Plastic-Eating Enzymes

プラスチック汚染は，今日の世界における主要な環境問題の一つであり，それに対する取り組みは，政府や科学者にとっての優先事項となっています。近年，研究者たちは，この問題にアプローチする新しい方法を考え出しました。それはプラスチックを「食べる」ことのできる酵素です。その仕組みを見てみましょう。

Key Vocabulary

次の単語について，その定義を結びつけましょう。

1. trash   **(a)** to throw away, get rid of

2. dispose of   **(b)** garbage, waste

3. comprise   **(c)** to reduce into smaller parts

4. break down   **(d)** an official right to make or sell an invention

5. dozen   **(e)** a group of twelve of the same thing

6. application   **(f)** the practical use of something

7. patent   **(g)** to make up, account for

2-36

It feels good to recycle, doesn't it? Every time we separate our trash into burnable and non-burnable garbage, we're taking a small step toward cleaning up the planet. Aren't we? The unfortunate answer to that question is no. Globally, less than 10 percent of plastic is recycled. About 12 percent of the 400 million tons of plastic waste produced
5 each year is burned, which is both energy intensive and polluting, while the rest is simply thrown away, piling up in landfill sites or the sea. The reason for this is that most packaging is made up of more than one type of plastic, which means it cannot be put to a new use. And even items made of only one kind of plastic are not always recyclable. The plastic used in yogurt cups, for instance, turns into a dark and smelly material,
10 making it hard for waste plants to deal with.

2-37

Finding an environmentally friendly way of disposing of plastic waste is, therefore, a priority both for governments and scientists. Recently, researchers at the University of Texas in the U.S. announced a new method for dealing with the problem: an enzyme that can "eat" plastic. The enzyme works on PET, a material found in most consumer
15 packaging, which comprises 12 percent of all global waste. Like all plastics, PET is made up of long string-like molecules. The enzyme reduces these molecules into smaller parts before chemically putting them back together so they can be recycled. In some cases, the plastics break down in just 24 hours, a process that in the oceans can take centuries.

2-38

Researchers have named their discovery FAST-PETase since it was developed from a
20 natural enzyme known as PETase. The team used artificial intelligence to generate genetic mutations to the enzyme, identifying which mutations would be most effective at breaking down plastic at a relatively low temperature of 50 degrees Celsius. They tested the new enzyme on dozens of items including containers, water bottles, and fibers, with experiments proving its success.

2-39

25 "This work really demonstrates the power of bringing together different disciplines from synthetic biology to chemical engineering to artificial intelligence," says Andrew

Ellington, one of the team members. He is confident the new method could have an enormous impact on not only the waste management industry but every sector of the economy, enabling companies to take a lead in recycling their own products.

 2-40

30 The next step for the researchers is scaling up production of the enzyme to prepare for industrial and environmental applications. They have already registered a patent that will allow it to be used to reduce the amount of waste in landfill sites. The team is also looking at ways to get the enzyme out into the environment to clean up polluted sites. The hope is that one day enzymes like FAST-PETase will solve the problem of plastic

35 waste completely.

Notes

landfill site ゴミ処理場, ゴミ埋め立て地 **enzyme** 酵素, エンザイム
genetic mutation 遺伝的変異 **discipline** 学問分野, 領域
synthetic biology 合成生物学 **sector** （経済）部門

True / False

次の文が本文の内容と一致する場合は T, 一致しない場合は F を記入しましょう。

1. (   ) More than 90 percent of plastic is not recycled.

2. (   ) Most packaging is constructed of a single type of plastic so it cannot be recycled.

3. (   ) FAST-PETase breaks down and reassembles PET molecules.

4. (   ) The University of Texas team came from a variety of different academic fields.

5. (   ) The research team is planning to expand production of the enzyme.

次の質問に英語で答えましょう。

1. How is about 12 percent of plastic waste disposed of now?

_____

_____

2. How long does it take FAST-PETase to break down plastics in some cases?

_____

_____

3. What legal document have the team applied for so they can use the enzyme in landfill sites?

_____

_____

Vocabulary in Context

次の英文の空所に入れるのに正しい語句を下から選びましょう。

1. There are a (　　　　　) reasons why this plan will not work.

2. We will need a (　　　　　) if we want to make profit from this invention.

3. This discovery has so many potential (　　　　　).

4. It is difficult to (　　　　　) industrial chemicals safely.

5. Oxygen (　　　　　) about 21 percent of the air.

| dispose of | comprises | dozen | applications | patent |

Writing Sentences — Expressing Preferences

好みを表す表現を学びます。次の英文の（　）内の単語を並べ替えて，意味の通る文にしましょう。
大文字の語も小文字で記されています。

1. 可能な限り，プラスチック製ではなく，紙製のストローを使用したい。

When possible, I (than / paper / to / a / straw / prefer / use) a plastic one.

(　　　　　　　　　　　　　　　　　　　　　　　　　　　　　　　　　)

2. スーパーマーケットは，お客様がマイバッグを持参することを望んでいる。

The supermarket would (own / customers / their / bring / rather) bags.

(　　　　　　　　　　　　　　　　　　　　　　　　　　　　　　　　　)

3. 企業には包装にプラスチックをあまり使わないでほしい。

I (not / companies / use / prefer / to / would) so much plastic in their packaging.

(　　　　　　　　　　　　　　　　　　　　　　　　　　　　　　　　　)

Listening Summary

 2-41

音声を聞いて，次の英文の空所を埋めましょう。

When you ¹⁾_____, you might think you are helping to save
the environment. Unfortunately, the truth is that only a small percentage of plastic is
²⁾_____. Most packaging is made up of more than one type
of plastic, ³⁾_____ cannot be reused; and some kinds of
plastic cannot be recycled at all. Recently, scientists at the University of Texas have
come up with a new way of ⁴⁾_____. They have genetically
engineered an enzyme that can "eat" PET, a material which comprises 12 percent of
⁵⁾_____. Known as FAST-PETase, the enzyme breaks down
the molecules of PET before putting them back together to enable recycling. It can do
so in ⁶⁾_____ 24 hours. By scaling up production of the
enzyme, the research team aims to use their product in landfill sites and polluted
areas.

A. クラスメートと話し合って，円の中にあるテーマに関係している単語をリストアップしてみましょう。

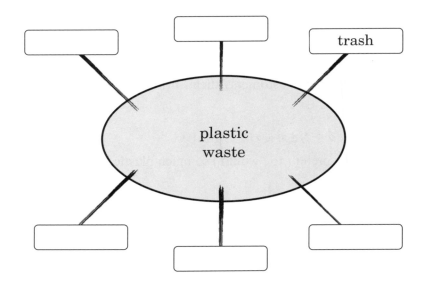

trash

plastic
waste

B. 次の英文を読んで，自分の考えを書きましょう。

1. Have you ever bought something and felt the packaging used too much plastic? What was it?

_____

_____

_____

2. How can we reduce the amount of plastic we use in our daily lives?

_____

_____

_____

UNIT 19 *No More Noisy Neighbors*

Soundproof Wallpaper

騒音公害は，最も深刻な環境被害の一つです。近年，科学者たちは，この問題に対する新しいアプローチ方法を発見しました。なんと蛾という非常に意外な生き物からインスピレーションを得たのです。蛾が防音壁紙の開発にどのように役立つのでしょうか。

次の単語について，その定義を結びつけましょう。

1. abnormal   (a) an animal that kills and eats other animals

2. branch   (b) a group of animals of the same type

3. predator   (c) a part of an academic field

4. echo   (d) made by humans

5. species   (e) the rate at which a wave vibrates

6. frequency   (f) a sound reflected back from an object

7. artificial   (g) different from or worse than normal

2-43

Have you ever had a noisy neighbor? The kind of person who plays their music at twice the normal volume, has parties when you're trying to sleep, or just seems to talk in an abnormally loud voice? If so, you're not alone. Noise pollution is the second largest environmental cause of health problems, just after the impact of air quality. Studies have
5 connected noise pollution to conditions including high blood pressure, heart disease, sleep loss, and stress. Fortunately, however, scientists have made a discovery that might put such problems in the past: soundproof wallpaper.

2-44

The miraculous wallpaper is based on copying a technology found in nature, a branch of science known as *biomimicry*. In this case, the technology is that of moth wings. Moths
10 might not be everyone's favorite living creatures, but they have evolved sophisticated methods of survival, in particular with regard to one of their natural predators, bats. Bats hunt using *echolocation*, which involves sending out sound waves and receiving the echoes reflected back from the target. To protect themselves from this method of attack, certain species of moth have evolved scales on their wings that absorb sound and so
15 make it difficult for bats to locate them. Scientists at the University of Bristol in the U.K. have been examining these scales to see whether they can be put to human use.

2-45

The team placed small sections of moth wings on an aluminum disk and systematically tested how sound absorption was affected by different noises and the direction they came from. "What we needed to know first was how well these moth scales would
20 perform if they were in front of an acoustically reflective surface such as a wall," explained Marc Holderied, one of the leaders of the study. Remarkably, the scales proved to be highly effective, absorbing up to 87 percent of the sound energy. They worked over a wide range of wave frequencies coming from a variety of angles.

2-46

What is even more impressive is that the scales are incredibly thin, just one fiftieth of the
25 wavelength of the sound they were absorbing. Their lightness means they could be valuable not only in wallpaper but also in modes of transport like planes, cars, and trains,

where the more weight you can cut in soundproof materials, the more fuel you save and the less carbon dioxide you emit.

 2-47

It should be pointed out that at the moment the team has only tested the moth wings
30   with ultrasound signals, which are above the frequency range that can be heard by humans. The researchers are confident, however, that they will be able to use the principles of the scales to design artificial versions which work at lower frequencies while remaining just as thin and light. "Moths are going to inspire the next generation of sound-absorbing materials," Professor Holderied says. Soon your neighbors might be
35   able to make all the noise they want.

Notes
blood pressure 血圧   **biomimicry** バイオミミクリー, 生物模倣
sophisticated 高度な   **echolocation** エコロケーション, 反響定位
scale 鱗粉, 鱗片   **acoustically** 音響的に   **wavelength** 波長
ultrasound 超音波

True / False

次の文が本文の内容と一致する場合は T，一致しない場合は F を記入しましょう。

1. (   ) Biomimicry means using human technology to change the environment.

2. (   ) Some moths have wings that are good at reflecting sound waves.

3. (   ) The research team needed to know whether moth scales would work when placed against a wall.

4. (   ) Moth wings could also be used to help airplanes fly more quickly.

5. (   ) Natural moth scales are not effective for sounds humans can hear.

次の質問に英語で答えましょう。

1. What is the largest environmental cause of health problems?

_____

_____

2. What method of hunting have moth wings evolved to prevent?

_____

_____

3. How thin are the moth scales compared to the sound waves they can absorb?

_____

_____

Vocabulary in Context

次の英文の空所に入れるのに正しい語句を下から選びましょう。

1. The government constructed an (   ) island in the sea.

2. This radio picks up a range of different (   ).

3. The tiger is perhaps the most dangerous (   ) of all.

4. If you shout your name on this mountain, you can hear a perfect (   ).

5. It is a comparatively new (   ) of science that is attracting a lot of attention.

branch	predator	echo	frequencies	artificial

Writing Sentences — Indirect Questions

間接疑問文を学びます。次の英文の（　）内の単語を並べ替えて，意味の通る文にしましょう。
大文字の語も小文字で記されています。

1. 研究者たちは，蛾に人間が活用できる秘密があるのでないかと考えた。

The researchers (moths / if / a / wondered / secret / held) that humans could make use of.

(　　　　　　　　　　　　　　　　　　　　　　　　　　　　　　　　　　)

2. 鱗片がどれだけの周波数を吸収できるかを調べた。

They (the / many / frequencies / how / scales / investigated) could absorb.

(　　　　　　　　　　　　　　　　　　　　　　　　　　　　　　　　　　)

3. 音波が吸収されるため，コウモリは蛾がどこに隠れているかを見つけることができない。

Because the sound waves are absorbed, bats (are / where / cannot / moths / hiding / find).

(　　　　　　　　　　　　　　　　　　　　　　　　　　　　　　　　　　)

Listening Summary

🎵 2-48

音声を聞いて，次の英文の空所を埋めましょう。

Noisy neighbors can cause sleep loss, stress, and [1]_____,
but what if there was a way to make the wallpaper in your apartment soundproof?
Recently, scientists at the University of Bristol have turned to a surprising source for
inspiration: moths. Some [2]_____ have evolved scales on
their wings that can [3]_____ in order to prevent bats using
echolocation to find them. The research team placed these scales on an aluminum disk
and [4]_____ to absorb sound waves coming at various
frequencies and angles. They found that up to 85 percent of the waves were absorbed
despite the scales being extremely [5]_____. So far, they have
only tested the scales on high-frequency ultrasound, which cannot be heard by
humans. But they are confident they can use the same principles to design
[6]_____ that will work at lower frequencies.

Express your Ideas

A. クラスメートと話し合って，円の中にあるテーマに関係している単語をリストアップしてみましょう。

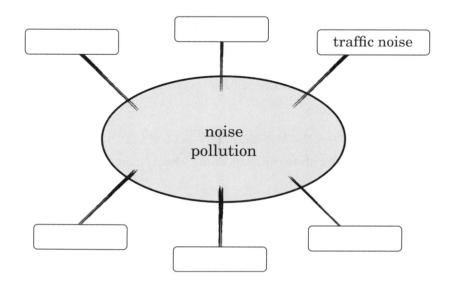

B. 次の英文を読んで，自分の考えを書きましょう。

1. Is your neighborhood noisy? Do you think noise pollution is a serious problem in Japan?

   _____

   _____

   _____

2. Soundproof wallpaper is based on biomimicry. What other ideas in nature would you like to copy?

   _____

   _____

   _____

Space Planes

Tokyo to Los Angeles in One Hour

残念なことに，現在の旅客機の速度は，60 年前と比べて少しも速くなっていません。しかし，その事実に変化が起きるかもしれません。現在，音速の 9 倍ものスピードで旅客機を飛ばす新技術が開発されているのです。どのような仕組みなのでしょうか。

Key Vocabulary

次の単語について，その定義を結びつけましょう。

1. atmosphere   (a) enough

2. obstacle   (b) a situation that makes it difficult to achieve something

3. air resistance   (c) to deal with or solve a problem

4. withstand   (d) the mixture of gases above Earth

5. sufficient   (e) normal, ordinary

6. conventional   (f) to be strong enough not to break

7. tackle   (g) the force that slows you down as you move fast

2-50

The idea of high-speed travel has been around for a long time. Back in the 1990s, a passenger aircraft named Concorde could take you from London to New York in three and a half hours by traveling at 2,179 km/hr or twice the speed of sound. But after a fatal crash in 2000, Concorde was retired and since then passengers have had to be satisfied
5 with a much slower pace of travel. Passenger jets today travel no faster than they did in the 1960s.

2-51

In the next decade or so, however, that might be set to change. Several companies are working on technology that will make even Concorde seem slow. They aim to create passenger planes that can travel not at twice the speed of sound but up to nine times, far
10 faster than even the most high-tech fighter planes can currently manage. The technology is based on using next-generation rocket engines to take aircraft to the edge of Earth's atmosphere, just 50 kilometers from space. Known as hypersonic planes, at their maximum speed of Mach 9, they could get you from Tokyo to Los Angeles in just one hour.

2-52

15 Naturally, there are many obstacles to overcome in order to reach such incredible speeds. There is the massive heat generated by air resistance, which requires new materials strong enough to withstand it but sufficiently light to allow the craft to fly. There are issues with maneuverability, navigation, and communication, all of which become far more difficult at hypersonic speeds.

2-53

20 And then there is the engine. Conventional rockets use a combination of fuel and oxygen to generate thrust. The oxygen, carried on board in liquid form, is particularly heavy, significantly increasing the amount of energy required to lift the rocket off the ground. Hypersonic engines propose to solve this problem by taking oxygen directly from the air, feeding it at high speed into the hydrogen fuel. The difficulty with this method is the
25 dangerously high temperature reached by the air as it passes into the engine, an issue the latest designs tackle with a new kind of coolant that is able to reduce the temperature by 1000 degrees Celsius in just one twentieth of a second.

2-54

Airbreathing engines will allow hypersonic planes to take off like a conventional aircraft with wheels and wings, so they can be reused after each trip. Of course, they will not be
30 as large as commercial aircraft. Most designs are based on holding a dozen passengers. As for the cost of a flight, the companies aim to charge around the price of a normal first-class ticket, at least eventually. For those that can afford it, the future promises a world where they can wake up in Tokyo, have lunch in Paris, and watch an evening show on Broadway in New York, not bad for a day's entertainment.

Notes

hypersonic ハイパーソニック，極超音速
Mach マッハ（超音速の速さを表す単位）　**maneuverability** 操作性
thrust 推力　**coolant** 冷却剤

True / False

次の文が本文の内容と一致する場合は T，一致しない場合は F を記入しましょう。

1. (　　　) Passenger jets today fly about as fast as they did in the 1960s.

2. (　　　) Hypersonic planes will fly in space.

3. (　　　) Conventional rockets have to carry heavy liquid oxygen inside the aircraft.

4. (　　　) Airbreathing engines need to be able to cool the oxygen for the engine extremely quickly.

5. (　　　) Eventually hypersonic planes should be the same size as normal passenger planes.

....

次の質問に英語で答えましょう。

1. Why is Concorde no longer in operation?

_____

_____

2. Why are new materials required for hypersonic planes?

_____

_____

3. How much is a ticket for a hypersonic plane predicted to cost eventually?

_____

_____

Vocabulary in Context

....

次の英文の空所に入れるのに正しい語句を下から選びましょう。

1. We need to (　　　　　　) this issue before it becomes too serious.

2. The (　　　　　) in this room is not very friendly.

3. It will not be (　　　　　) to study only the night before the test.

4. The team was not able to (　　　　　) the pressure created by their opponents.

5. This new machine should work more quickly than a (　　　　) type.

atmosphere	withstand	sufficient	conventional	tackle

Writing Sentences—Indirect Speech

間接話法を学びます。次の英文の（　　）内の単語を並べ替えて，意味の通る文にしましょう。
大文字の語も小文字で記されています。

1. 会社は新型のエンジンを開発したと発表した。

The company (had / developed / they / a / announced) new kind of engine.

(　　　　　　　　　　　　　　　　　　　　　　　　　　　　　　　　　　　　)

2. 科学者は，極超音速飛行機が実現するには，あと 10 年はかかると予測した。

The scientist (another / it / predicted / take / decade / would) for hypersonic planes to

become a reality.

(　　　　　　　　　　　　　　　　　　　　　　　　　　　　　　　　　　　　)

3. チケットの価格が下がることを期待している。

We (tickets / price / expect / of / the / that / will) decrease.

(　　　　　　　　　　　　　　　　　　　　　　　　　　　　　　　　　　　　)

Listening Summary CD 2-55

音声を聞いて，次の英文の空所を埋めましょう。

Since the retirement of Concorde after a crash in 2000, 1)_____

have maintained the same speed they had in the 1960s. In the next 10 to 20 years,

however, that might finally change. A 2)_____ of rocket

engines is being developed that could power aircraft far beyond current speeds, even

to 3)_____ nine times the speed of sound. Rockets depend on

mixing fuel with oxygen to create thrust. But while 4)_____

have to carry the oxygen on board, the new engines take it directly from the air. This

allows them not only to cut weight but also to have wheels and wings like a normal

plane. Flying at such high speeds is 5)_____ – there are

issues of heat, maneuverability, navigation, and communication that all have to be

solved. Nevertheless, scientists are confident that hypersonic planes might soon

6)_____. Fancy having your lunch in Los Angeles today?

Express your Ideas

A. クラスメートと話し合って，円の中にあるテーマに関係している単語をリストアップしてみましょう。

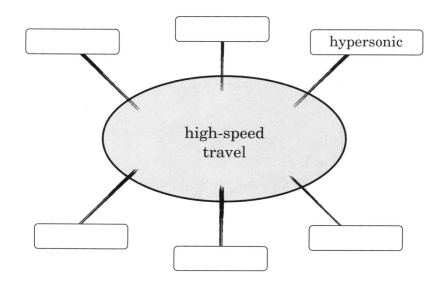

B. 次の英文を読んで，自分の考えを書きましょう。

1. What is your favorite type of transport (airplanes, trains, cars, buses etc.)? Why?

_____

_____

_____

2. If you could fly on a hypersonic plane, where would you like to go in one day?

_____

_____

_____

Key Vocabulary

- abnormal (adj.)
- absorb (vb.)
- accelerate (vb.)
- accomplish (vb.)
- adapt (vb.)
- affect (vb.)
- agility (n.)
- air resistance (n.)
- alter (vb.)
- anesthesia (n.)
- anxiety (n.)
- appetite (n.)
- application (n.)
- artificial (adj.)
- asteroid (n.)
- astronomy (n.)
- atmosphere (n.)
- attract (vb.)
- bacteria (n.)
- bandage (n.)
- benefit (n.)
- branch (n.)
- break down (vb.)
- breakthrough (n.)
- capable of (adj.)

- cell (n.)
- civilization (n.)
- collaboration (n.)
- colleague (n.)
- colonize (vb.)
- come up with (vb.)
- compete (vb.)
- complex (adj.)
- component (n.)
- comprise (vb.)
- conscious (adj.)
- conservation (n.)
- constant (adj.)
- consumption (n.)
- contribute (vb.)
- conventional (adj.)
- decline (vb.)
- definition (n.)
- deforestation (n.)
- delay (n.)
- detect (vb.)
- determine (vb.)
- digestion (n.)
- dispose of (vb.)
- diversity (n.)

- dozen (n.)
- echo (n.)
- ecosystem (n.)
- emissions (n.)
- enable (vb.)
- encounter (vb.)
- endangered species (n.)
- equator (n.)
- estimate (vb.)
- evaluate (vb.)
- evolve (vb.)
- exaggeration (n.)
- exclamation (n.)
- extinction (n.)
- extract (vb.)
- factor (n.)
- fatal (adj.)
- feline (adj.)
- fleet (n.)
- fluid (n.)
- frequency (n.)
- function (n.)
- gene (n.)
- generate (vb.)
- habitat (n.)

- ❏ herbivore (n.)
- ❏ hostile (adj.)
- ❏ identify (vb.)
- ❏ ill-effect (n.)
- ❏ immune (adj.)
- ❏ inequality (n.)
- ❏ initiate (vb.)
- ❏ inject (vb.)
- ❏ interaction (n.)
- ❏ launch (n./vb.)
- ❏ legal (adj.)
- ❏ livestock (n.)
- ❏ loyal (adj.)
- ❏ manufacture (n.)
- ❏ meteorite (n.)
- ❏ mimic (vb.)
- ❏ miniature (adj.)
- ❏ molecule (n.)
- ❏ morally (adv.)
- ❏ mosquito (n.)
- ❏ observe (vb.)
- ❏ operation (n.)
- ❏ orbit (n./vb.)
- ❏ organ (n.)
- ❏ overcome (vb.)

- ❏ patent (n.)
- ❏ phenomenon (n.)
- ❏ pollution (n.)
- ❏ precise (adj.)
- ❏ predator (n.)
- ❏ pregnant (adj.)
- ❏ preserve (vb.)
- ❏ primitive (adj.)
- ❏ principle (n.)
- ❏ quality (n.)
- ❏ quantity (n.)
- ❏ obstacle (n.)
- ❏ odor (n.)
- ❏ regulation (n.)
- ❏ reptile (n.)
- ❏ resource(s) (n.)
- ❏ rule out (vb.)
- ❏ saliva (n.)
- ❏ satellite (n.)
- ❏ soil (n.)
- ❏ solar system (n.)
- ❏ solution (n.)
- ❏ species (n.)
- ❏ sprout (vb./n.)
- ❏ sterile (adj.)

- ❏ stroke (vb.)
- ❏ subside (vb.)
- ❏ sufficient (adj.)
- ❏ suppress (vb.)
- ❏ scarce (adj.)
- ❏ surgery (n.)
- ❏ survival (n.)
- ❏ sustain (vb.)
- ❏ tackle (vb.)
- ❏ threaten (vb.)
- ❏ time-consuming (adj.)
- ❏ trash (n.)
- ❏ vital (adj.)
- ❏ wealth (n.)
- ❏ withstand (n.)

Section I:
Nature and the Environment
Memo

UNIT 1

UNIT 2

UNIT 3

UNIT 4

UNIT 5

UNIT 6

UNIT 7

UNIT 8

UNIT 9

UNIT 10

UNIT 11

UNIT 12

UNIT 13

UNIT 14

UNIT 15

UNIT 16

Section V:
The Future Now
Memo

UNIT 17

UNIT 18

UNIT 19

UNIT 20

TEXT PRODUCTION STAFF

| edited by | 編集 |
| Minako Hagiwara | 萩原 美奈子 |

| English-language editing by | 英文校閲 |
| Bill Benfield | ビル・ベンフィールド |

| cover design by | 表紙デザイン |
| Nobuyoshi Fujino | 藤野 伸芳 |

| text design by | 本文デザイン |
| Nobuyoshi Fujino | 藤野 伸芳 |

CD PRODUCTION STAFF

narrated by	吹き込み者
Neil DeMaere(AmerE)	ニール・デマル（アメリカ英語）
Jennifer Okano(AmerE)	ジェニファー・オカノ（アメリカ英語）

Science Inspirations
未来を創る科学の英知

2024年1月10日　初版印刷
2024年1月20日　初版発行

著　　者　Dave Rear

発 行 者　佐野 英一郎

発 行 所　株式会社 成美堂
　　　　　〒101-0052　東京都千代田区神田小川町3-22
　　　　　TEL 03-3291-2261　FAX 03-3293-5490
　　　　　https://www.seibido.co.jp

印 刷・製 本　倉敷印刷株式会社

ISBN 978-4-7919-7287-6　　　　　　　　　Printed in Japan